ABSOLUTELY EVERYTHING YOU NEED TO KNOW

ABSOLUTELY EVERYTHING YOU NEED TO KNOW

Written by
SIMON HUGO

CONTENTS

CHAPTER ONE

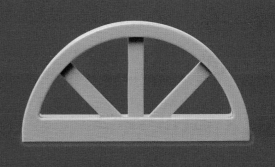

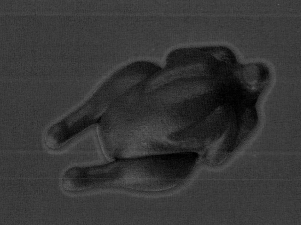

BRICKS AND PIECES

BEFORE THE BRICK

In the years before LEGO® bricks, the LEGO Group made a wide selection of toys, first crafted from wood, and then from plastic.

WOW!

The wooden LEGO Tractor from 1949 may look basic, but it has functional front-wheel steering, just like a LEGO® Technic set.

FACT STACK

The LEGO Group founder, Ole Kirk Kristiansen, crafted his first wooden toys in 1932.

The first playthings to be sold bearing the LEGO brand name were produced in 1934.

Wooden LEGO toys of the 1930s included the first-ever LEGO cars and trains.

The LEGO Group made its first plastic toys in 1947, alongside its range of wooden items.

REALLY?!

When a craze for wooden yo-yos ended, the LEGO Group turned its leftover stock into colorful wheels for other toys!

Q | Are there any wooden LEGO bricks?

A | No—but there were wooden LEGO blocks. From 1946, stackable cubes were made for early learners. They were painted with brightly colored letters and numbers.

TOP 5

Pull-along wooden LEGO toys

1 **Duck** opens and closes his beak.

2 **Clumsy Hans** bobs up and down.

3 **Monkey** rocks back and forth.

4 **Dog** turns his head and wags his tail.

5 **Chickens** peck the ground in turn.

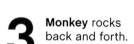

▌AWESOME!

One of the first sets to feature plastic playing pieces, Monypoli was a 1948 board game with squares that spelled out the word "LEGO."

28

Wooden toys were listed in Ole Kirk Kristiansen's first product catalog in 1932, including a fire truck, a race car, and an airplane.

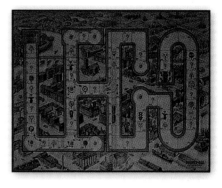

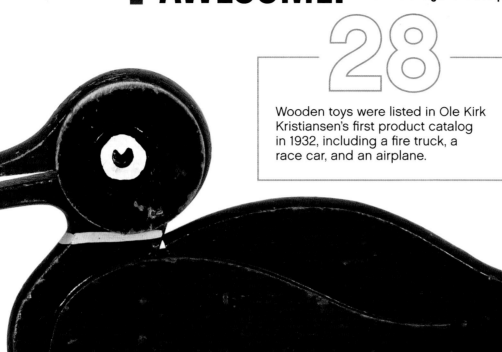

Brick History

One of the most popular early LEGO toys, 1935's wooden LEGO Duck was recreated as a modern, brick-built LEGO set in 2011 and given to LEGO Group employees as a Christmas gift.

BRICK CHALLENGE

Choose your favorite from the toys shown here, then make a 21st-century version using your LEGO bricks.

PLASTIC PLAYTIME

Some of the first plastic LEGO toys included a baby's rattle shaped like a fish and a sailor figure that could slide down a rope.

IT'S A SIGN!

As a mark of quality and authenticity, most wooden LEGO toys were labeled with a sticker showing an early LEGO logo and proudly proclaiming "BILLUND DENMARK."

SANDBOX GAME

The first LEGO construction toy was Kirk's Kuglebane ("Kirk's Ball Track," also known as "Kirk's Sand Game"). Released in 1935, it comprised small wooden blocks that could be arranged in a sandbox to make a track for a metal ball.

GET WITH THE SYSTEM

Conceived in 1955, the simple but innovative idea that every plastic LEGO element should be part of a wider "System" is still at the heart of LEGO building today.

KEY DATES

1949
The company's first plastic bricks are sold as "Automatic Binding Bricks." They have studs on top, but no tubes underneath, and slits on two sides.

1953
Automatic Binding Bricks are officially renamed "LEGO Bricks" ("LEGO Mursten" in Danish). The LEGO name is molded onto each stud for the first time.

1955
The LEGO System in Play launches with the LEGO Town Plan: 28 LEGO brick building sets plus eight vehicles, all designed to be used together.

1957
Tubes are built into the underside of LEGO bricks so that they clutch securely to the studs on top of the one below. The new bricks go on sale in 1958.

1958
Stud-and-tube interlocking is one of several brick-building systems covered by the LEGO brick patent, awarded on January 28.

Brick History

In 1954, Godtfred Kirk Christiansen came up with the idea for the LEGO System in Play when the chief buyer for a major Danish department store complained that the toy industry had "no system of any kind!"

FACT STACK

Since 1955, the majority of LEGO sets have been part of the LEGO System in Play.

The LEGO System in Play means that LEGO sets never become obsolete.

The LEGO System in Play is divided into different "themes" that are all compatible.

Modern LEGO System themes include LEGO® NINJAGO®, LEGO® City, and LEGO® Friends.

WOW!

Lots of prototype pieces were made to perfect the "clutch power" that fastens LEGO bricks together without making them too hard to pull apart.

915,103,765

The number of ways that six classic 2x4 LEGO bricks of the same color can be combined.

AWESOME!

Today's 2x4 LEGO bricks have exactly the same measurements as the ones made in the 1950s. They will fit perfectly with any brick from the past 60 years.

1

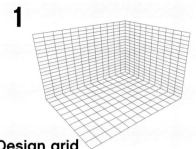

Design grid

2

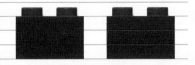

One brick,
three plates

3

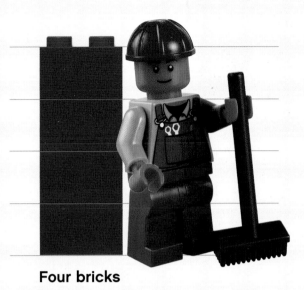

Four bricks

ON THE GRID

1 To ensure all elements fit in the LEGO System in Play, new LEGO parts are designed according to a three-dimensional grid.

2 Making sure all LEGO elements align within the grid increases the potential for parts to serve more than one function—in future sets or simply in creative play.

3 Even specialized pieces such as minifigures and accessories must conform to the grid. This ensures they can connect with other pieces in as many ways as possible.

BRICK CHALLENGE

There are 24 ways to combine two 2x4 LEGO bricks. See if you can find them all!

Q What are LEGO bricks made from?

A Until 1963, LEGO bricks were made from cellulose acetate. Since then, they have been made from a different type of plastic—acrylonitrile butadiene styrene (ABS)—which is more durable and colorfast.

WOW!

When a LEGO Technic pin is inserted into a LEGO Technic hole, it makes a sound that LEGO employees refer to as a "rewarding click!"

REALLY?!

In 2009, there were thought to be 62 LEGO bricks for every person in the world. Today, the estimate stands at 102!

Piece particulars

Some LEGO elements are named after the designer that made them. The Erling brick is one of them, named after LEGO Designer Erling Dideriksen who invented this element in 1979.

MAKING PLANS

Before LEGO "themes" as we know them today, Town Plan sets were the first LEGO products to combine small, brick-built models into an ever-growing urban scene.

ELEMENT ESSENTIALS

Right from the early days of LEGO sets, there have been especially useful LEGO elements to help you build in various different ways. Many of those are still around today. Here are 25 bricks and pieces that really put the fun in fundamentals.

Start here!

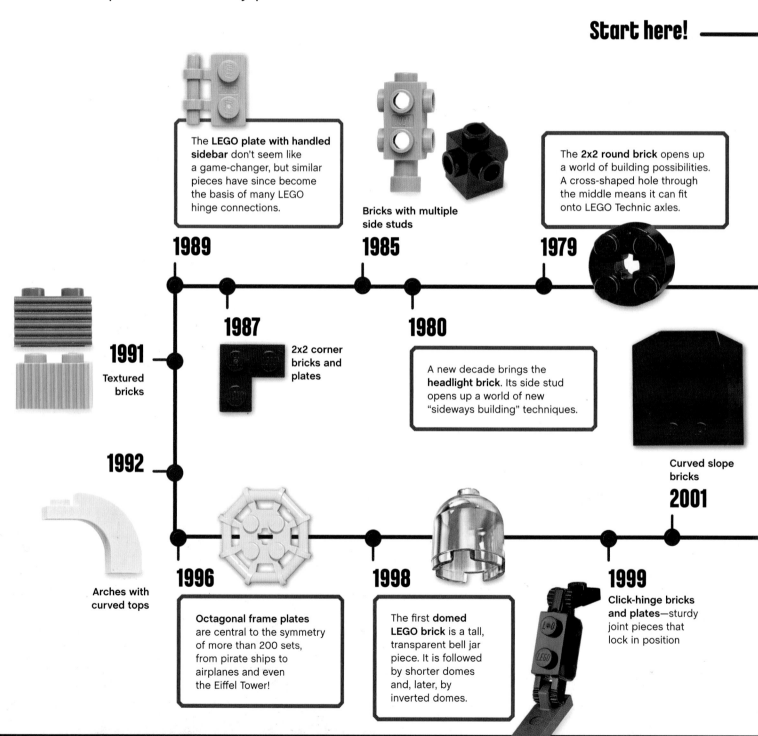

The **LEGO plate with handled sidebar** don't seem like a game-changer, but similar pieces have since become the basis of many LEGO hinge connections.

1989

Bricks with multiple side studs

1985

The **2x2 round brick** opens up a world of building possibilities. A cross-shaped hole through the middle means it can fit onto LEGO Technic axles.

1979

1991

Textured bricks

1987

2x2 corner bricks and plates

1980

A new decade brings the **headlight brick**. Its side stud opens up a world of new "sideways building" techniques.

Curved slope bricks

2001

1992

Arches with curved tops

1996

Octagonal frame plates are central to the symmetry of more than 200 sets, from pirate ships to airplanes and even the Eiffel Tower!

1998

The first **domed LEGO brick** is a tall, transparent bell jar piece. It is followed by shorter domes and, later, by inverted domes.

1999

Click-hinge bricks and plates—sturdy joint pieces that lock in position

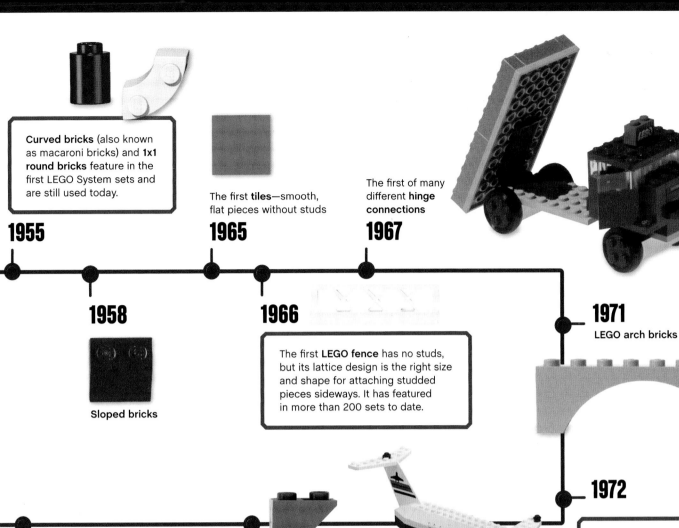

Curved bricks (also known as macaroni bricks) and **1x1 round bricks** feature in the first LEGO System sets and are still used today.

1955

The first **tiles**—smooth, flat pieces without studs

1965

The first of many different **hinge connections**

1967

1958

Sloped bricks

1966

The first **LEGO fence** has no studs, but its lattice design is the right size and shape for attaching studded pieces sideways. It has featured in more than 200 sets to date.

1971

LEGO arch bricks

1972

Builds go sky high with the introduction of **wedge-shaped plates** for aircraft wings. More than 40 different angled plates have been produced since.

1978

The **jumper plate** allows other pieces to "jump" the regular pattern of LEGO building and sit halfway between two studs. It has featured in almost 2,000 sets.

1976

Inverted slope bricks

1x1 round plates with holes

2009

2014

2004

Tooth plates are so called because they look like fangs. They are also great for making claws and for adding architectural details.

2013

Round tiles with holes

The LEGO® Mixels™ theme puts a new spin on **LEGO ball-and-socket** couplings. The latest connectors not only move in any direction but also stay in position once posed.

2017

More than 30 years after the first bricks with side studs, a **brick with side studs on two adjacent sides** only is launched. It's perfect for adding details on corners.

TALLEST TIRE

The LEGO® Technic CLAAS XERION 5000 TRAC VC tractor (set 42054) has tires that measure a whopping 4.21in (107mm) in diameter.

REINVENTING THE WHEEL

One good turn deserves another, and there's always a new LEGO wheel rolling into view! Here are the top tires and weirdest wheels...

AWESOME! The most wheels on an individual vehicle (not including trains and trucks with trailers) is 14 on the LEGO City Cargo Plane (set 7734) From 2008.

TOP 5

Wheels that make the LEGO world go round

1 Steering wheel (1978)

2 Cartwheel (1985)

3 Ship's wheel (1985)

4 Fancy carriage wheel (2014)

5 Wheelchair wheel (2016)

HEAVIEST TIRE

The heaviest LEGO tires were made for the LEGO Technic Power Puller (set 8457). Each 6oz (170g) tire weighs more than 150 standard LEGO City car tires.

WOW!

LEGO City Tire Escape (set 60126) features one large tire but no wheels. It is used as a boat by an escaping crook!

730,000,000+

Number of LEGO tires produced in 2016, making the LEGO Group one of the world's biggest tire manufacturers.

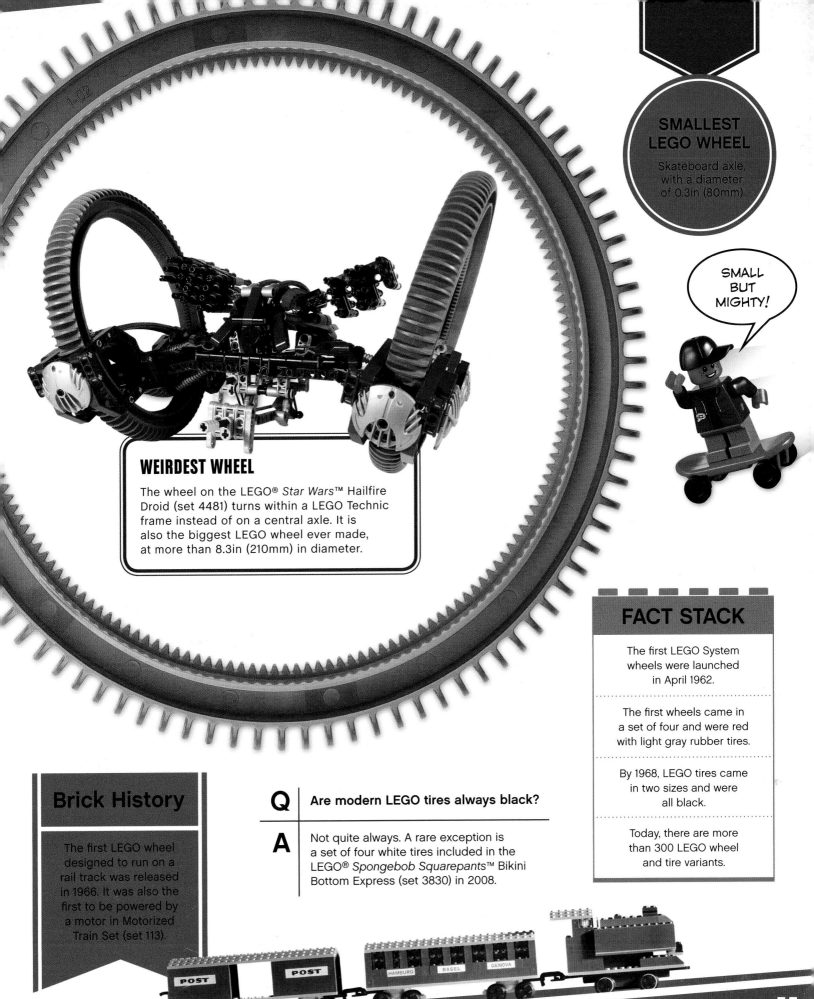

SMALL
BUT
MIGHTY!

WEIRDEST WHEEL

The wheel on the LEGO® Star Wars™ Hailfire
Droid (set 4481) turns within a LEGO Technic
frame instead of on a central axle. It is
also the biggest LEGO wheel ever made,
at more than 8.3in (210mm) in diameter.

FACT STACK

The first LEGO System
wheels were launched
in April 1962.

The first wheels came in
a set of four and were red
with light gray rubber tires.

By 1968, LEGO tires came
in two sizes and were
all black.

Today, there are more
than 300 LEGO wheel
and tire variants.

Brick History

The first LEGO wheel
designed to run on a
rail track was released
in 1966. It was also the
first to be powered by
a motor in Motorized
Train Set (set 113).

Q | Are modern LEGO tires always black?

A | Not quite always. A rare exception is
a set of four white tires included in the
LEGO® Spongebob Squarepants™ Bikini
Bottom Express (set 3830) in 2008.

POST   POST   HAMBURG   BASEL   GENOVA

THE LEGO® COLOR CHART

CLASSIC COLORS

These six classic colors have been used in LEGO® sets for over 50 years.

Bright Red (LEGO color number: 21)

Bright Yellow (24)

White (1)

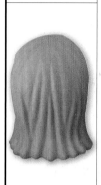

Dark Green (28)

Bright Blue (23)

Black (26)

Cool Yellow (226)

Bright Orange (106)

Flame Yellow Orange (191)

Bright Purple (221)

Light Purple (222)

Bright Red Violet (124)

Light Royal Blue (212)

Medium Blue (102)

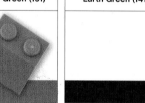

Sand Blue (135)

Earth Blue (140)

Sand Green (151)

Earth Green (141)

Bright Yellow Green (119)

Olive Green (330)

Reddish Brown (192)

Nougat (18)

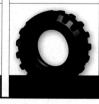

Light Nougat (283)

Dark Orange (38)

Medium Stone Gray (194)

Transparent Yellow (44)

Transparent Bright Orange (182)

Transparent Fluorescent Red Orange (47)

Transparent Red (41)

Transparent Medium Violet (113)

Transparent Bright Violet (126)

Transparent Blue (43)

Transparent Fluorescent Blue (143)

LEGO elements have been made in more than 150 shades since the 1950s. Some colors have come and gone, including solid neons and shades with glitter. This rainbow of color covers hues that are currently in production.

New Dark Red (154)

Medium Lavender (324)

Lavender (325)

Medium Lilac (268)

Dark Azur (321)

Medium Azur (322)

Spring Yellow Green (326)

Aqua (323)

Bright Green (37)

Brick Yellow (5)

Sand Yellow (138)

Medium Nougat (312)

Dark Brown (308)

Dark Stone Gray (19

Tran
Light

METALLIC AND EFFECT COLORS

The first metallic colors appeared in the 1970s. There are four metallic and effect colors currently in production.

Titanium Metallic (316)

Warm Gold (297)

White Glow (329)

Silver Metallic (315)

The L
UFO Int
Starfighte
is one of the
feature fiber-optic cab
light up with an eerie al

colors, and more,
rs, including
alistic builds.

2002

Send any **LEGO®**
Spybotics set on a
undercover missior
and it will follow
your programmed
instructions, using
light and touch
sensors to find it

Transparent Brown (111)

Transparent (40)

TRANSPARENT COLORS

Transparent elements joined the LEGO color palette in the late 1960s.

THE PATH TO POWER

Lots of electrical innovations have brought light, sound, and movement to LEGO sets over the years, culminating in today's "Power Functions."

New "Code Pilot" technology emerges in **LEGO Technic Barcode Multi-Set** (set 8479). Scanning special barcodes controls the speed, sound, and actions of this motorized tipper truck.

Start here!

The **LEGO® MINDSTORMS® sets** appear. They use infrared technology to send instructions from your home computer to "smart bricks" built into a range of robots.

1998

1998

With instructions for building five powered cars, **Radio Control Racer** (set 5600) is the first set to come with a wireless remote-control unit.

The LEGO® Studios theme launches with a **digital camera** built like a large LEGO element. The camera can be fixed into place for making stop-motion LEGO movies.

1997

EGO® Space
terstellar
_r_ (set 6979)
only sets to
es, which
ien glow.

2000

The compact **LEGO Technic Speed Computer** (set 5206) appears, allowing you to measure the speed, travel time, and distance covered by your vehicle builds.

Electric light comes to LEGO sets with the first **light-up brick**. A replaceable bulb inside the transparent 2x4 brick connects to a 4.5-volt battery.

1957

The first **battery-powered LEGO motor** is launched in North America. Wheels attach directly to the transparent "Motor Pak," which has studs on top for building.

1965

New 4.5-volt motors herald the arrival of **powered LEGO trains**. The motors can also be fitted with tires instead of train wheels for building motorized cars.

1966

The **LEGO Technic Control Center** (set 8094) offers the power to build four programmable machines, including a robot arm and a drawing device.

The **LEGO® Light and Sound System** adds working sirens and flashing LED lights to Town and Space sets, powered by the first 9-volt LEGO battery boxes.

1977

The first **LEGO Technic sets** are released with instructions on how to motorize them using the more compact 4.5-volt motor designed for this theme.

1990

1986

The first sound bricks with built-in batteries add va-va-VROOOM to eight different motorbike builds in **LEGO® Creator Revvin' Riders** (set 4893).

The dawn of **LEGO Power Functions** marks the start of a whole new era of battery-powered functionality in 21st-century LEGO sets.

2006

2003

2007

A new, unique memory module in **LEGO Creator Record and Play** (set 4095) remembers how you moved a model, and then replays those movements!

Since 2007, the LEGO Group has used "Power Functions" motors and other special elements to animate and illuminate sets in ways never seen before.

Big machines

Grand Carousel (set 10196)

3,263 pieces
Including a Power Functions motor

13.8in (35cm) high
And 15in (38cm) across

8 LEGO Technic camshafts
Make the ride rise and fall as it turns

6 AA (1.5V) batteries
Hidden beneath ride operator's platform

1 sound brick
Plays music as the carousel turns

Q | **Can Power Functions be added to any LEGO set?**

A | Anything is possible with a little imagination! But to get you started, a few sets come with instructions for adding Power Functions, such as the LEGO® Mars Mission MT-61 Crystal Reaper (set 7645) from 2008.

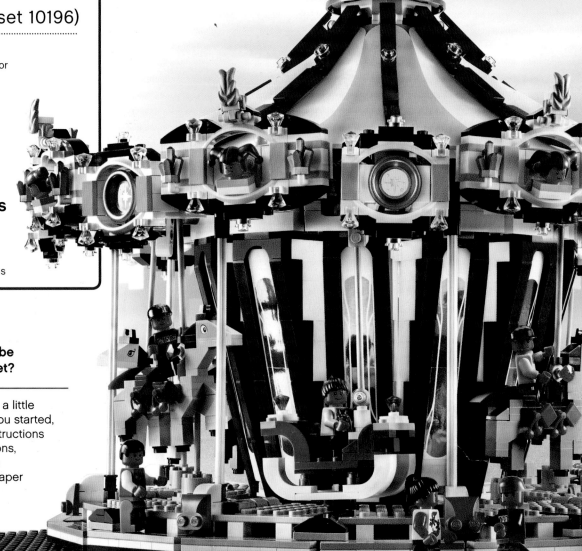

AWESOME!

The 2007 LEGO Creator Monster Dino (set 4958) can walk, wield its claws, bare its fangs, and ROAR!

TOP 5

Sets with special light bricks

1 Winter Toy Shop (set 10199)

2 Fiery Legend (set 6751)

3 Rescue Robot (set 5764)

4 UFO Abduction (set 7052)

5 Lighthouse Point (set 31051)

20,000

Number of unique license plates created for the limited-run LEGO Technic Power Functions 4x4 Crawler Exclusive Edition (set 41999) in 2013.

EK 00001 of 20000

FACT STACK

Most LEGO Power Functions motors are just six studs long and three studs wide.

More than 20 LEGO Technic sets have featured Power Functions motors since 2007.

A Power Functions motor with built-in steering features in just two 2009 LEGO Racers sets.

Since 2010, all LEGO City Trains have run on special Power Functions motors.

THIS RIDE HAS REAL HORSE POWER!

WOW!

The 2010 LEGO Technic Motorized Excavator (set 8043) uses four Power Functions motors—for driving, turning, digging, and lifting.

Brick History

In 2008, a limited edition Wind Turbine (set 4999) was produced in partnership with Danish renewable energy firm Vestas. The set included a Power Functions motor to make its rotors spin.

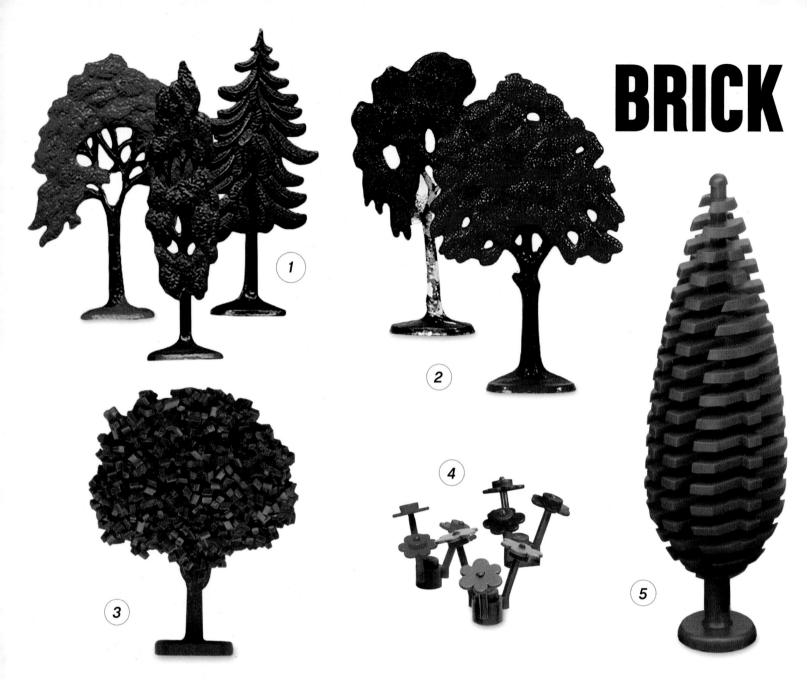

Notable plants and flowers of the LEGO world

1 **Trees and Bushes (set 230).** Rare; these trees were designed to add greenery to the LEGO Town Plan theme of the 1950s, but could not be built onto other elements.

2 **Trees and Bushes (set 490).** Rare; in the mid 1960s, LEGO trees were redesigned with bases that could be built onto other elements, but retained their detailed, real-world look.

3 **Fruit tree from Trees and Signs (set 990).** Rare; most LEGO elements are made from tiny granules of ABS plastic that are heated and shaped in a mold. For this 1970s LEGO tree, those granules were only partially melted to create a unique look.

4 **Flowers.** Widespread; the most abundant and diverse flora in the LEGO biosphere, LEGO flowers bloom most commonly in red, but also in blue, yellow, white, and four shades of pink.

5 **Cypress tree.** Rare; dating back to the time of the first LEGO® Castle sets, this tree was found in just a handful of sets in the 1980s.

BOTANY

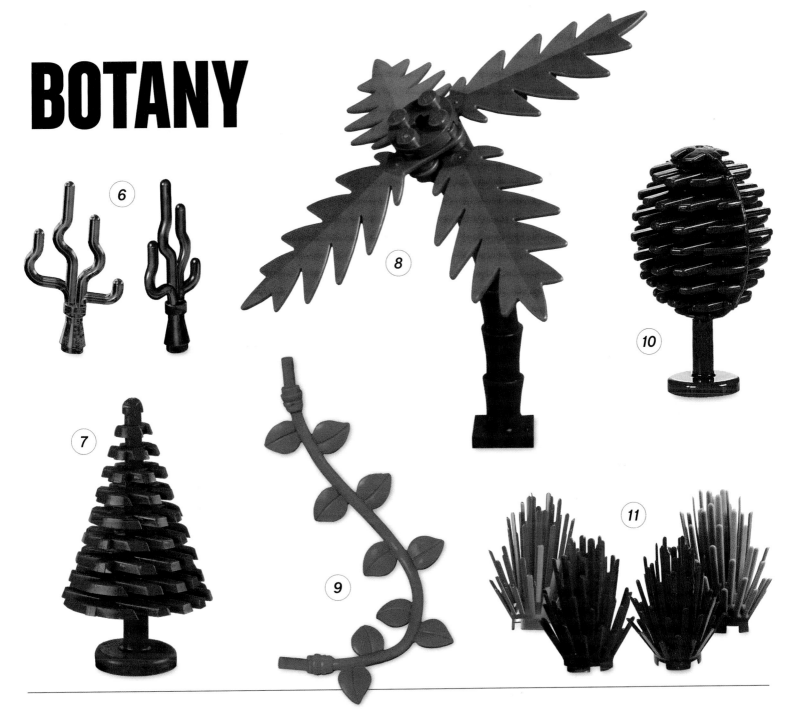

6   **Sea grass.** Widespread; frequently found in underwater habitats, but also seen on mountains, in parks, and on islands.

7   **Pine tree.** Widespread; the most common LEGO tree appears in over 100 sets. A hardy evergreen, it is also found snow-capped in two discontinued wintry sets.

8   **Palm tree.** Widespread; originally limited to tropical areas frequented by LEGO® Pirates, a variety with shorter leaves (pictured) has since been found in Heartlake City, home of LEGO® Friends.

9   **Leafy vine.** Restricted; recently discovered by LEGO® botanists, this flexible vine has been established in Heartlake City.

10 **Fruit tree.** Relict; once a familiar sight in LEGO Town and LEGO City, this fruit tree was last seen in 2010. A scarce lime variety was found in one Creator set in 2013.

11 **Prickly bush.** Widespread; this adaptable shrub has been noted in at least 120 locations, mostly in green but also in tan, dark tan, and red.

1977

Also known as Expert Builder Sets, the first Technical Set models include a forklift truck, a tractor, and a helicopter.

1984

The LEGO Technic theme name appears on boxes for the first time, and the first pneumatic sets use compressed air pumps to power machine functions.

1990

The battery-powered Control Center (set 8094) brings basic programming functionality to LEGO Technic sets for the first time.

1999

A forerunner of LEGO BIONICLE, the LEGO Technic Slizer subtheme (known as Throwbots in North America) stars disk-throwing alien robots!

2007

Remote-controlled Power Functions add new electronic features to larger LEGO Technic sets. Motorized Bulldozer (set 8275) was the first, and won the Nuremberg Innovation Award.

2017

Celebrating 40 years of LEGO Technic, this vehicle can be built using pieces from three LEGO Technic sets (42057, 42061, and 42063), with instructions available at LEGO.com.

Q Why do most LEGO Technic beams have an odd number of holes when most LEGO bricks have an even number of studs?

A Because any beam with an odd number of holes will always have a connecting point right in the middle—and combining two such beams still allows for even-numbered lengths.

Brick History

In 1996, the first LEGO Technic studless beam appeared in Space Shuttle (set 8480). Today, studless beams have largely replaced brick-style beams in LEGO Technic sets.

LOOK CLOSER

Not all LEGO Technic pins are created equal! Black and blue pins have extra ridges so that they make a tighter connection than gray and tan-colored ones.

WOW!

The LEGO Technic Star Wars Destroyer Droid (set 8002) uses rubber bands to spring into attack mode when you roll it along!

AWESOME!
More than a dozen LEGO Technic sets feature pullback motors so they can speed into action without needing batteries.

Brick statistics

90+ LEGO Technic cars
From go-karts to F1 racers

50+ construction vehicles
Diggers, cranes, dozers, and more

40+ trucks and tractors
One of which turns into a robot!

35+ motorcycles
Including trikes and ATVs

30+ airplanes and helicopters
Plus a single space shuttle

FACT STACK

The first LEGO gears came out in 1965. They are not compatible with LEGO Technic elements.

There are more than 20 types of LEGO Technic gear, counting rack and pinion elements.

LEGO® BIONICLE® elements were originally designed as part of the LEGO Technic theme.

Today, many large LEGO sets rely on LEGO Technic beams and connectors at their cores.

40

Teeth on the largest LEGO Technic gearwheel.

TOP 5

Essential LEGO Technic elements

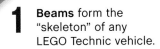

1 **Beams** form the "skeleton" of any LEGO Technic vehicle.

2 **Pins** connect beams and other parts at any angle.

3 **Axles** slot through beams to connect moving parts.

4 **Gears** are wheels with teeth that turn on axles.

5 **Bushes** space out elements and hold axles in place.

Piece particulars

Since 1991, flexible rods have added curves to LEGO Technic sets—sometimes for functional reasons, and sometimes just to look cool!

LET'S GET TECHNICAL

Over the past 40 years, budding engineers have been using LEGO Technic elements to build bigger, more complex models full of moving parts and working mechanisms.

IT'S A SIGN!

Every LEGO Technic set released in 2017 comes with a special printed beam celebrating the theme's 40th anniversary.

40
1977–2017

LEGO® HOMEMAKING

Doors

(1)

(2)

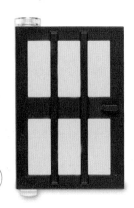

(3)

(4)

Windows

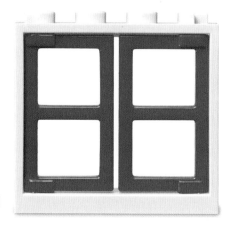

(1)

(2)

(3)

(4)

1. **Door with four panes.** This iconic shape was introduced in 1978 and updated in 2008.

2. **Arched door.** This rounded door shape emerged in 2001 for the launch of the LEGO® *Harry Potter*™ theme.

3. **Door with six panes.** This right-handed door appeared in over 20 sets from 1983. A left-handed version came with one 1984 set: Cargo Center (set 6391).

4. **Door with stud handle.** This door builds into a corner at an angle. It often appears in LEGO Creative loose-brick boxes, to help fans build their own homes.

1. **Classic.** Technically three pieces (two panes and a frame), this is the most common LEGO window shape.

2. **Lattice.** This old-world-style window has been made in 15 colors. It can even be found in pink.

3. **Panel.** A clear panel clicks into this simple window frame. Some sets come with colored panes or stickers on the panel.

4. **Fanlight.** This curved window was inspired by classical-style architecture. It appeared in LEGO sets from 2015.

Fences

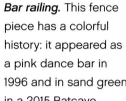

1 ***Picket fence.*** It is no surprise that white is the most common color for this piece.

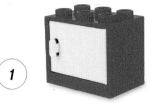

2 ***Bar railing.*** This fence piece has a colorful history: it appeared as a pink dance bar in 1996 and in sand green in a 2015 Batcave.

3 ***Spindled fence.*** In 2003, this fence with four top studs replaced a version with two studs— one on each end.

4 ***Lattice fence.*** A true classic, the 1x4x1 fence panel has been in production since 1966.

5 ***Ornamental fence.*** This decorative piece was first found in the fantastical world of LEGO® Elves in 2015.

Finishing touches

1 ***Cupboard.*** These simple cupboards have provided storage for minifigures for more than 30 years.

2 ***Drawer.*** Featuring the same basic box element as the cupboard, drawers also help to keep LEGO homes tidy.

3 ***Mixer faucet.*** This decorative faucet has added style to kitchens and bathrooms since 2002.

4 ***Mailbox.*** These hinged elements can also be found in sets as fridges, ovens, or even as part of a longcase clock.

PLENTY OF PIECES

There are several ways to define the biggest LEGO set, but the most common way is to count the number of pieces a set contains. These LEGO behemoths are the five most piece-heavy sets ever.

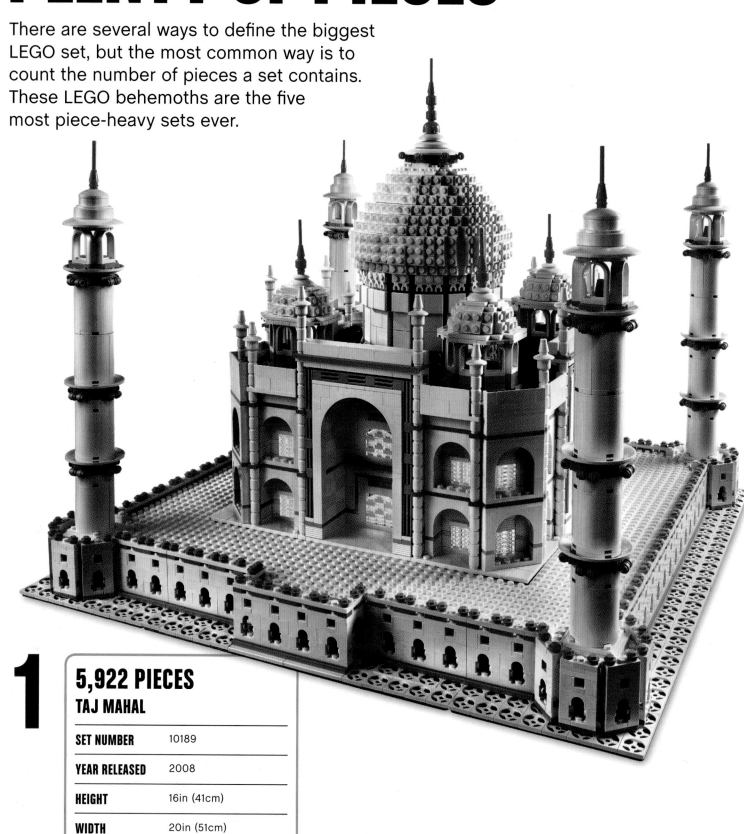

1

5,922 PIECES

TAJ MAHAL

SET NUMBER	10189
YEAR RELEASED	2008
HEIGHT	16in (41cm)
WIDTH	20in (51cm)

3

4,634 PIECES
LEGO® *GHOSTBUSTERS*™: FIREHOUSE HEADQUARTERS

SET NUMBER	75827
YEAR RELEASED	2016
HEIGHT	14in (36cm)
LENGTH	14in (36cm)

2

5,197 PIECES
ULTIMATE COLLECTOR'S *MILLENNIUM FALCON*

SET NUMBER	10179
YEAR RELEASED	2007
WIDTH	12in (32cm)
LENGTH	33in (84cm)

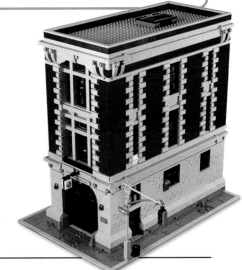

4

4,295 PIECES
TOWER BRIDGE

SET NUMBER	10214
YEAR RELEASED	2013
HEIGHT	17in (43cm)
LENGTH	40in (102cm)

5

4,163 PIECES
BIG BEN

SET NUMBER	10253
YEAR RELEASED	2016
HEIGHT	23in (60cm)
LENGTH	17in (43cm)

Fun and games

1 **Teddy Bear.** Since accompanying Sleepyhead from the LEGO® Minifigures line to bed in 2012, the Teddy Bear has brought comfort to minifigures in many sets.

2 **Paintball gun.** The Paintballer's gun is a unique piece, molded especially for him in LEGO Minifigures Series 10.

Sports

3 **Ski poles.** These ski poles are most commonly found in white, but they were also made in pearl gold to top the turrets of the LEGO Big Ben set (set 21013) in 2016.

4 **Barbell weights.** The weights of this barbell accessory are used by minifigures in training, but is also used as a LEGO vehicle hubcap.

Music

5 **Acoustic guitar.** In 2016, the Serenader was the first minifigure to play an acoustic guitar. His maraca-playing bandmate also debuted his instrument.

6 **Violin case.** There is a violin case LEGO accessory but no violin! The Gangster carries the case around—who knows what he keeps inside it!

Tools of the trade

7 **Plunger.** Only two minifigures carry plungers: Groundskeeper Willie from *The Simpsons* LEGO Minifigures series and the Plumber, who has his hands full servicing other LEGO homes.

8 **Paint roller.** The paint roller piece can be fitted to any 1x1 round brick to change the paint color. The Decorator first used this with a light blue piece in 2013.

ASSORTED

ACCESSORIES

Aids to sight

9   *Magnifying glass.* The transparent lens of the magnifying glass actually works, enhancing the sight of minifigures and builders alike.

10   *Binoculars.* One of the most common LEGO accessories, binoculars appear in over 300 sets. The Lifeguard is the only minifigure to hold them in red.

Tech

11   *Laptop.* There is only one model of laptop available to minifigures, in three colors—black, dark bluish gray, and dark purple. There are nine different stickers for laptop screens.

12   *Camera.* This black camera is usually found capturing the adventures of minifigures. The only red version can be found in THE LEGO® BATMAN MOVIE Arkham Asylum (set 70912), released in 2017.

Printed material

13   *Newspaper.* Whether it's the *Zombie Times Braaains!* cookery column or *City Financial News* piece on stud growth, minifigures can keep up to date with the latest LEGO news items with printed newspaper tile pieces.

14   *Map.* Minifigures can navigate their way to treasure or the town hall with the variety of printed map pieces that are available in the LEGO world.

Miscellaneous

15   *Short bone.* Bones are popular among the canine LEGO population and a few minifigures have taken a shine to them, too. The Cave Woman and LEGO NINJAGO villain Lord Garmadon wear them as hair pieces.

16   *Coins.* Until 2011, LEGO currency came in 10, 20, 30, and 40 pieces. In sets produced after this they were in 1, 2, 5, and 10 pieces.

NICE PART USE

Finding a familiar piece and then using it in an unexpected way is called nice part use, or "NPU," by some LEGO fans. These NPUs prove there is never just one use for any LEGO element!

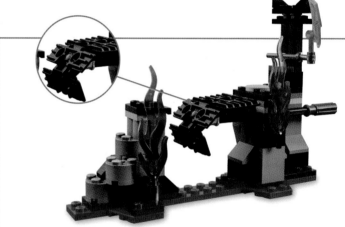

The Alien Mothership (set 7065) from 2011's LEGO Space Alien Conquest theme uses eight pieces of **railway track** to create its saucer shape.

Torts (set 41520) from 2014's LEGO® Mixels™ range has **starfish** for hands, a **roof piece** for a nose, and **wheel arches** for eyebrows.

A piece of **caterpillar track** becomes a perilous twisting bridge in LEGO® NINJAGO® Lava Falls (set 70753) from 2015.

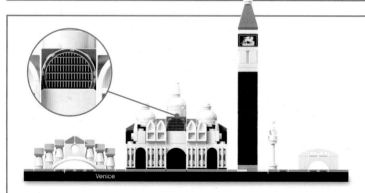

In 2016's LEGO® Architecture Skyline of Venice (set 21026), a printed round tile more often used as a lowly **air vent** becomes the huge, semi-circular window of St Mark's Basilica.

Some fairly bruised-looking **banana pieces** make horns for Burnzie the Lava Monster in the 2016 LEGO® NEXO KNIGHTS™ set Axl's Tower Carrier (set 70322).

A **flag piece** makes an unlikely appearance in the bathroom of LEGO Friends Summer Riding Camp (set 3185)—as a toilet seat cover!

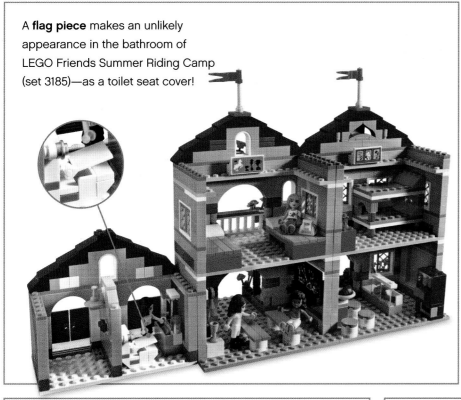

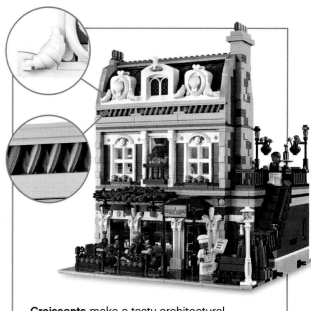

Croissants make a tasty architectural detail above a row of **feather pieces** in 2014's Parisian Restaurant (set 10243) from the LEGO® Creator Expert Modular Buildings theme.

The LEGO Creator Expert Big Ben (set 10253) from 2016 uses **minifigure tools** for clock hands, **microfigures** designed for the LEGO® Games theme as statues, and **skeleton legs** as railings.

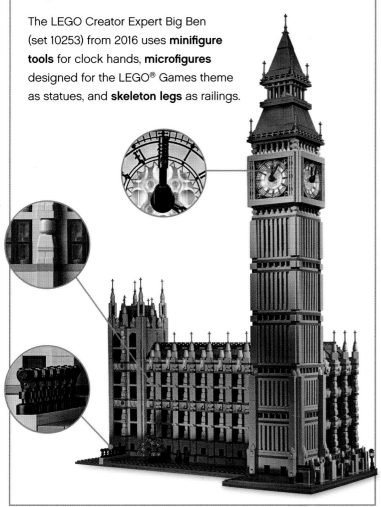

Assembly Square (set 10255) from 2017's LEGO Creator Expert Modular Buildings range has a roof made out of LEGO Technic **excavator buckets**.

CHAPTER TWO

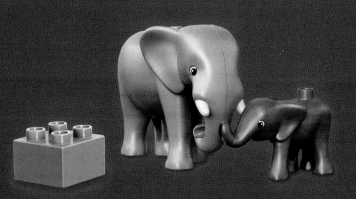

BUILDING

WORLDS

STARTING BLOCKS

LEGO® DUPLO® is a world of big building pieces for small hands. Since 1969, it has inspired generations of preschoolers to learn more about their environment through colorful, creative play.

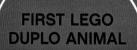

FIRST LEGO DUPLO ANIMAL

A dog in DUPLO Camping (set 536) in 1977

98,765,432,110

The biggest number you can build by moving around the numbered blocks in the DUPLO Number Train (set 10558).

IT'S A SIGN!

duplo

The friendly DUPLO rabbit logo was launched in 1979. In 1985, a fabric version of the rabbit was released—you could store your bricks inside it!

WE'RE HERE FOR ALL YOUR PET EMERGENCIES.

▌AWESOME!

In Batman Adventure (set 10599), Batman, Superman, and Wonder Woman team up to rescue a cat from a river!

LOOK CLOSER

The 1980 set School and Bus (set 2645) has a clock with moving hands, a blackboard with interchangeable pictures, and a ringing bell.

Studs in scale

LEGO brick
Standard LEGO bricks are compatible with DUPLO bricks, but only when built on top of DUPLO bricks.

LEGO DUPLO brick
The name "DUPLO" comes from the Latin word for "double," because the dimensions of DUPLO bricks are twice the size of standard LEGO bricks.

Top 5

DUPLO worlds

1. Farm
2. Airport
3. Dino
4. Castle
5. Pirates

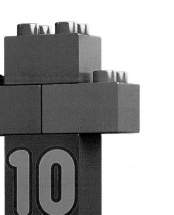

REALLY?!

The first-ever LEGO toilet appeared in 1986, in the DUPLO set Bathroom (set 2754).

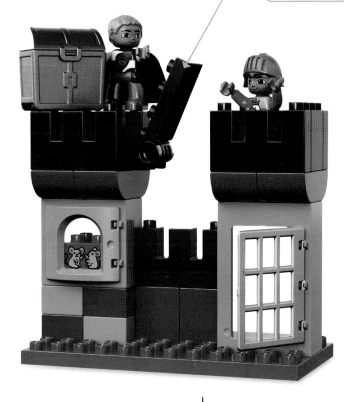

Q When did the LEGO DUPLO Zoo close?

A The Zoo theme was a firm favorite from 1990, but DUPLO animals have been released into the wild since 2009. They now appear in sets based on their natural environments, such as the Savannah, the Arctic, and the Jungle.

Brick History

The first DUPLO figures, released in 1977, had block-shaped bodies with no arms or legs, and heads that turned but were not detachable.

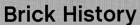

THE SIGHTS OF LEGO® CITY

There's lots to see and do in LEGO® City. To help visitors get the most out of their stay, this street plan shows some of the most well-known places around.

CITY MUSEUM

Jewels, swords, and paintings such as *Minifigure with a Pearl Earring* are just some of the sights to see (and for LEGO burglars to steal!) at this museum (set 60008).

USEFUL INFORMATION

GETTING AROUND
LEGO City is easily accessible with its range of buses, trams, trains, planes, and ferries.

DINING
There are endless dining options in LEGO City. Even the street vendors are smartly dressed chefs.

MAIL
The first LEGO Post Office (set 6362) opened in LEGO Town in 1982, and today mailboxes can be found across LEGO City.

BANKING
Cash can be withdrawn from the LEGO City Bank via ATM, or by stealing the safe with a bulldozer.

CITY PARK

Popular with dog walkers and cyclists, the Fun in the Park set (set 60134) is fully wheelchair-accessible and includes a picnic area.

WATERFRONT

See huge cranes and container ships at LEGO City Harbor (set 4645, pictured), then go surfing or sailing at the beachside marina (set 4644).

SPACEPORT

LEGO City has an extensive space program, so time your visit to take in a spectacular shuttle launch at the Spaceport (set 60080).

CITY SQUARE

Take the tram to the heart of the city and seek out the perfect souvenir at the two-story LEGO Store in City Square (set 60097).

> I WILL PROTECT YOU, FROGS.

TOWN SQUARE

Stop off at the bustling Town Square (set 60026) to admire this unusual statue of a knight surrounded by frogs.

PRISON ISLAND

This offshore jail (set 60130) can be seen from the harbor, so keep an eye out for daring escapes by balloon!

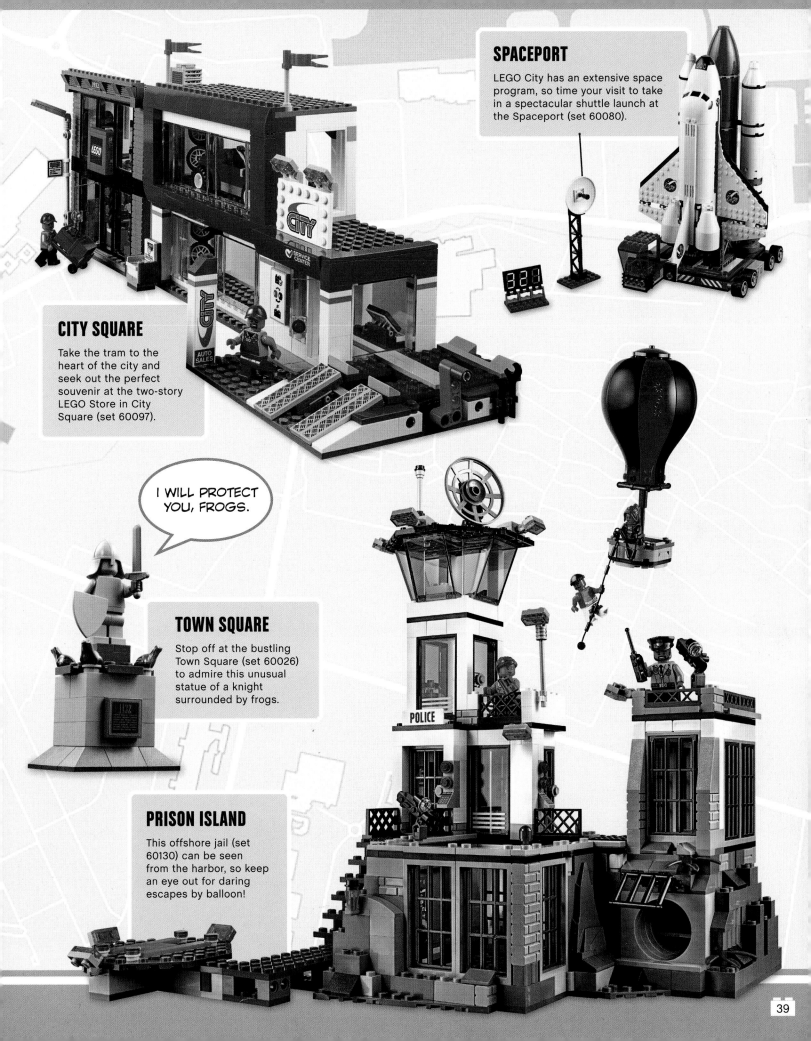

CALL THE COPS

The LEGO City police department keeps crooks at bay and kids at play. Happily, there's no height requirement to join!

TOP 5

Crook-catching police vehicles

1 Helicopters

2 Motorcycles

3 Boats

4 Airplanes

5 Patrol cars

Brick History

The first LEGO products to feature police elements were the Town Plan sets way back in 1955, which came with static traffic police.

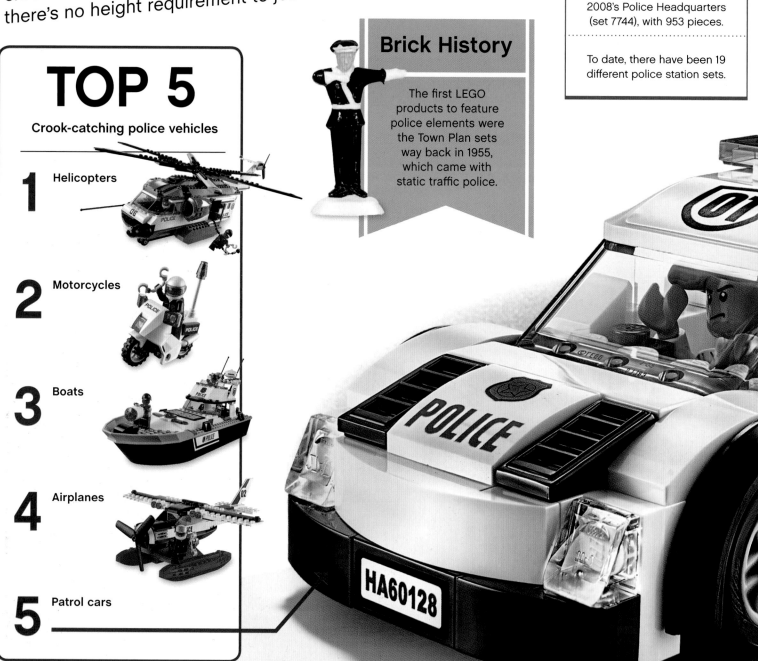

HA60128

▌ AWESOME!

1985's Mobile Police Truck (set 6450) was the first LEGO police vehicle to have flashing lights and a siren.

LOOK CLOSER

The Traffic Cop in the LEGO® Minifigures line can issue a parking ticket, and the signature on it is that of a real-life LEGO designer!

1973
The first police minifigure was also the first LEGO minifigure ever. He went on patrol with a stick-on uniform and a police car he couldn't fit into!

1980
The first female LEGO police officer came in a special set for schools. She had white hair that matched her open-topped patrol car.

1993
LEGO police officers got new-look uniforms as part of the LEGO Town Rescue theme, and featured individual face designs for the first time.

2012
The LEGO Forest Police sets saw officers in sun hats and tan-colored uniforms, dodging huge bears while riding dirt bikes in the woods.

REALLY?!
There were no LEGO crooks until 1993 and no LEGO handcuffs until 2008. What were the LEGO police doing for 20 years?!

CHASE BY NAME, CHASE BY NATURE!

CHASE ON THE CASE
Of all the LEGO police officers to appear in sets since 1978, the only one to be given an official name is Chase McCain, heroic star of the LEGO® City *Undercover* video games.

LOOK CLOSER

In Police Headquarters (set 7744), a bored crook has scrawled graffiti on the prison cell walls!

MOST WANTED

Have you seen any of these infamous LEGO crooks? Some of them have been causing trouble for the LEGO City police for years!

FUNNY HOW WE'RE ALL THE SAME HEIGHT.

First seen: 2016   First seen: 2015   First seen: 2017   First seen: 2005   First seen: 1993

IT'S A SIGN!
LEGO City police officers can be identified by the gold badges on their uniforms. These sometimes feature a star with four brick-style studs.

WHAT'S COOKING?

Brick History

The food on offer in 1990's Breezeway Café (set 6376) and Pizza To Go (set 6350) proved so popular the sets were re-released in 2002 as LEGO® Legends sets.

CAFÉ CULTURE

Café Corner (set 10182), was the first-ever LEGO® Modular Building in 2007. It is a great place for minifigures to grab a snack and watch the world go by.

Even LEGO minifigures get hungry! Luckily, there are many LEGO restaurants with all kinds of foods on the menu.

TOP 5

Abundant fruit and vegetables in the LEGO world

 1 Apple, appears in more than 110 sets.

2 Carrot, appears in more than 95 sets.

 3 Turkey drumstick, appears in more than 85 sets.

 4 Cherries, appears in more than 80 sets.

 5 Banana, appears in more than 75 sets.

Q Can I order pizza by the slice in LEGO City?

A Of course! The Pizza Van (set 60150) was the first set to offer individual pizza slices, but you can also order a whole pizza if you are hungry enough...

WOW!

The LEGO® Friends theme was the first to use a decorated minifigure head as a pineapple in LEGO sets!

Piece particulars

LEGO ice cream comes in 11 different flavors. Vanilla must be the most popular—white ice-cream scoops have appeared in 31 sets.

IT'S A SIGN!

This takeaway coffee cup, seen in THE LEGO® MOVIE™ and with Larry the Barista (set 71004), features the logo of The Coffee Chain, Brickburg's most expensive coffee shop.

SNACK BAR

1979
The first LEGO Snack Bar (set 675) opens in LEGO Town, serving ice cream, coffee, and more.

REALLY?!

LEGO chefs come in all shapes and sizes! There's even a robot chef named Chef Éclair, who appears in LEGO® NEXO KNIGHTS™ sets.

ANYONE FANCY A BYTE?

1980
LEGO Town citizens snack on fish and chips for the first time in LEGO Town Square Castle Scene (set 1592). The Dutch version of this set serves "soup und wurst!"

1983
A Hamburger Stand (set 6683) arrives in LEGO Town, serving burgers in the form of stacked 1x1 tiles!

1990
LEGO Town gets its first sit-down restaurant with the romantic-looking Italian eatery Breezeway Café (set 6376).

HOTEL

Piece particulars

LEGO minifigures have been enjoying hot-dog sausages since 1998, but they didn't get a bun to go with them until 2016!

LOOK CLOSER

The LEGO pizza slice is topped with green peppers, mushrooms, and olives. Yum!

ISLAND LIFE

2,028

The number of pieces in Temple of Airjitzu (set 70751), the largest LEGO® NINJAGO® set.

Welcome to Ninjago Island. The world of NINJAGO sets is one of powerful (LEGO) elements, varying landscapes, and battles between the forces of good and evil.

Piece particulars

The LEGO NINJAGO theme introduced a new LEGO element–an A-shaped plate–which has since become a builder favorite due to its versatility.

FACT STACK

The ninja and Master Wu protect Ninjago Island from evil forces.

The main elements of Ninjago Island are Fire, Ice, Earth, Lightning, and Water.

Ninjago Island and its neighboring country, Dark Island, form a yin-yang shape.

The capital of Ninjago Island is the hi-tech, high-rise Ninjago City.

AWESOME!

When their home was lost in a battle, the ninja moved into a wooden sailing ship called *Destiny's Bounty*. It can fly as well as float.

1 **Spinning katana swords** from Spinjitzu Dojo (set 2504).

2 **Mace ball** from Mountain Shrine (set 2254).

3 **Axe head spinner** from Mountain Shrine (set 2254).

4 **Serpentine sword post** from Ninja Training (set 30082).

5 **Spear target** from Ninja Training Outpost (set 2516).

Q Who created Ninjago Island?

A The first Spinjitzu Master created Ninjago Island by combining the four Golden Weapons. He wanted it to be a peaceful land of light, but he learned that light cannot exist without darkness. He became the island's first protector, guarding it against dark forces—just like the ninja do today.

WOW!

There are 14 realms, or dimensions, that are parallel to the Ninjago dimension. There used to be 16 before two were destroyed.

> I'M ON TOP OF THIS... ROOF!

Piece particulars

Flexible garage door panels create the distinctive curve on the roof of this smugglers' market, part of the Temple of Airjitzu (set 70751).

REALLY?!

The huge spider-like design on Garmadon's Dark Fortress is more than a terrifying architectural feature—it can jump off to attack unsuspecting ninja!

OUT OF THIS WORLD

The LEGO® Space theme blasted into orbit in the 1970s. Since then it has rocketed beyond our solar system to discover ice planets, space bugs, and more!

WOW!

Robotic space bugs from the planet Zotax brought a whole new buzz to LEGO Space in the 1998 Insectoids subtheme.

TOP 5

Astronaut space bases

SPACE BASE 1979 TO SPACE BASE 1988. OVER.

1 Command Center (set 926), 1979

2 Space Supply Center (set 6930), 1983

3 Message Intercept Base (set 6987), 1988

4 Space Station Zenon (set 1793), 1995

5 Space Police Central (set 5985), 2010

‖ AWESOME!

In 2007, the LEGO® Mars Mission subtheme used hand pumps to launch Martian figures through the base's transport tubes.

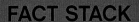

FACT STACK

The LEGO Space race began with four sets in 1978.

The LEGO Space theme got an update in 1987, with the dawn of "Futuron."

Since 1987, there have been 21 different Space subthemes.

Space subthemes include three versions of the popular LEGO® Space Police.

Q Are all LEGO Space sets based in outer space?

A No. The Alien Conquest subtheme, released in 2011, was based around an alien invasion of Earth—a first for LEGO Space.

FIRST FLYING SAUCER

Spyrius Gigantic Spy UFO (set 6939)

> HAPPY BIRTHDAY TO ME!

30

Years of LEGO Space was celebrated in 2009 with the release of this space minifigure statue in Galactic Enforcer (set 5974).

IN·ANNOS·TRIGINTA·
AD·CAELUM·INFINITUM·
CONSTRUXIT·

> THERE'S NO SPACE FOR CRIME HERE.

STOP, POLICE!

In 1989, the first LEGO Space Police brought Blacktron crooks to justice, locking them up in portable prison pods.

REALLY?!

In 1990, M:Tron sets used magnets to defy gravity. Magnetic elements would later feature in Ice Planet 2002 and Spyrius sets.

Brick History

In 1983, Galaxy Commander (set 6980) boasted a feature that would define many future Space sets: the ability to easily split into different builds.

MAKING HISTORY

Few eras in history are as fondly remembered and action-packed as the bygone age of LEGO® Castle, which included more than just LEGO castles!

FACT STACK

There have been more than 200 LEGO Castle sets since the theme launched in 1978.

The name LEGO Castle was not actually used on set packaging until 2007.

LEGO Castle Advent Calendars counted the knights until Christmas in 2008 and 2012.

14

Number of LEGO Castle sets that feature fire-breathing dragons!

IT'S A SIGN!

The huge shield in 2005's King's Siege Tower (set 8875) is one of the largest LEGO Castle elements. It includes a built-in LEGO brick, so you can add your own details to it.

REALLY?!

More than a decade before LEGO® NINJAGO®, 1990s LEGO Castle sets, such as Treasure Transport (set 6033), featured the very first LEGO ninja!

AWESOME!

The biggest-ever LEGO Castle set is not a castle at all, but the 1,601-piece Medieval Market Village (set 10193) from 2009.

CHECKERED HISTORY

Four LEGO Castle chess sets have been released since 2005, pitching knight against dragon, king against skeleton queen, dwarf against troll, and jester against wizard!

Brick History

In 2001, two much-loved 1980s sets, Guarded Inn (set 6067) and Black Falcon's Fortress (set 6074), were reissued as "LEGO Legends" sets for a whole new generation to enjoy.

LOOK CLOSER

In 1988, LEGO Castle horses wore decorative barding for the first time. From 2005, they sometimes wore armored headgear, too.

TOP 5

Pieces first found in LEGO Castle sets

1 Flags (1984)

2 Rocks (1992)

3 Flames (1993)

4 Bats (1997)

5 Cows (2009)

WOW!

In 1984, the LEGO Castle Catapult (set 6030) made use of LEGO® Technic parts to become the first missile-launching LEGO set!

HAVE YOU TRIED GETTING IN?

YES, IT MAKES THE KNIGHTS FLY BY!

CAPTURING THE CASTLES

In the Middle Ages, it took decades to build a decent castle. Since 1978, there have been scores of LEGO Castle sets that can be built within hours!

1984

New large wall panel pieces made for quicker castle building, and allowed for printed stonework details in sets such as **King's Castle** (set 6080).

1978

The first **LEGO Castle** (set 375) is unmistakable in bright yellow. Like many castles that followed, this set has hinged walls that open for easy play.

2009

The only LEGO Castle stronghold not to be controlled by knights, **Trolls' Mountain Fortress** (set 7097) has the Crown King guarded by enormous trolls.

2007

King's Castle Siege (set 7094) blended classic LEGO Castle looks with modern play features such as catapults, a collapsing wall, and a spinning bridge.

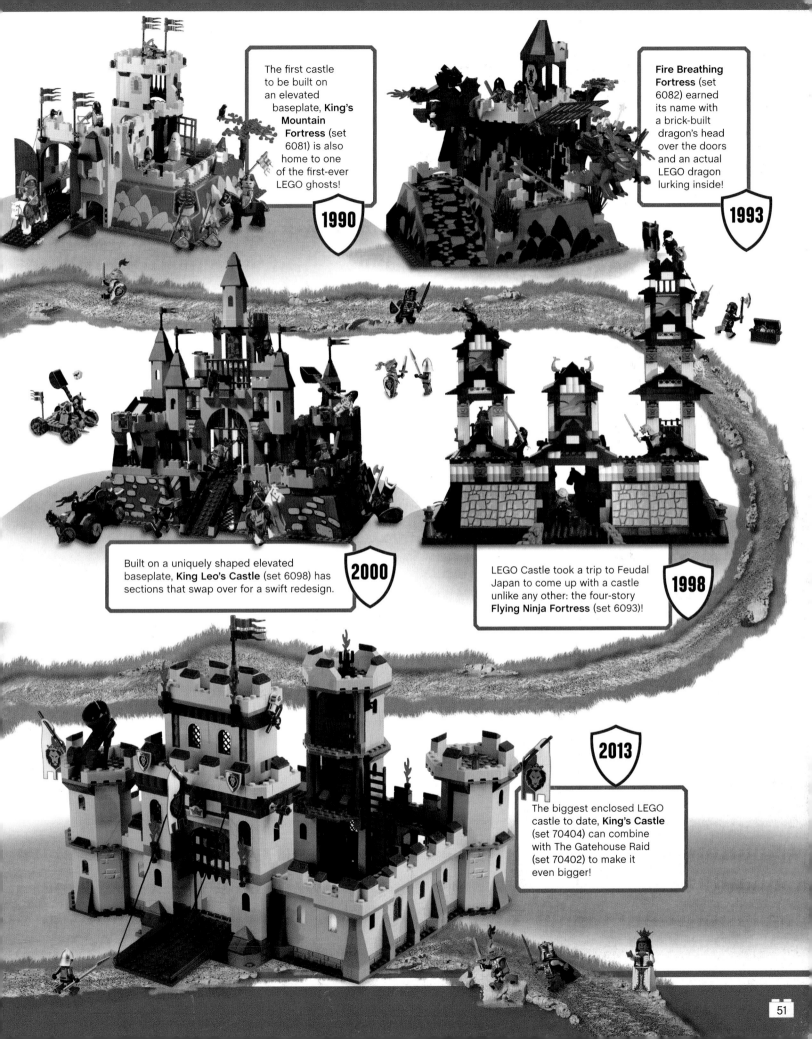

The first castle to be built on an elevated baseplate, **King's Mountain Fortress** (set 6081) is also home to one of the first-ever LEGO ghosts!

1990

Fire Breathing Fortress (set 6082) earned its name with a brick-built dragon's head over the doors and an actual LEGO dragon lurking inside!

1993

Built on a uniquely shaped elevated baseplate, **King Leo's Castle** (set 6098) has sections that swap over for a swift redesign.

2000

LEGO Castle took a trip to Feudal Japan to come up with a castle unlike any other: the four-story **Flying Ninja Fortress** (set 6093)!

1998

2013

The biggest enclosed LEGO castle to date, **King's Castle** (set 70404) can combine with The Gatehouse Raid (set 70402) to make it even bigger!

AHOY MATEY!

Avast ye landlubbers—be on the lookout, there be LEGO® Pirates about! For nearly 30 years this scurvy crew have been causing trouble across the seven seas.

FACT STACK

The LEGO Pirates theme was launched in 1989.

The LEGO Group has released close to 80 different LEGO Pirates sets.

There have been 10 LEGO Pirates galleon sets, representing various different fighting factions.

Unsurprisingly, more than 35 LEGO Pirates sets feature a treasure chest.

WHY ARE PIRATES CALLED PIRATES?

THEY JUST AARRR!

REDBEARD BY NAME...

LOOK CLOSER

Captain Redbeard and his crew, released in 1989, were the first minifigures to have extra facial details along with the classic LEGO smile.

KEY DATES

1989
The Bluecoat Imperial Soldiers are the first group to lose their valuable treasure to the Pirates.

1992
Next to try and guard their treasure against becoming pirate plunder are the Redcoat Imperial Guard.

1996
The Imperial Armada set out to hunt LEGO Pirates, but end up being looted instead!

2009
Having no respect for a new Imperial uniform, the Pirates begin stealing from Redcoat Imperials again.

2010
While traveling with Redcoat Imperials, the Governor's Daughter has to protect her treasure from the Pirates.

2015
The return of the classic Bluecoat Imperials provides updated but familiar faces to steal from.

IMPERIAL STRONGHOLD

Governor's Fort Sabre (set 6276) is home to the Pirates' arch-enemies, the Imperial Soldiers. This popular 1989 set features a fort, a dock, and a jail where captured Pirates are imprisoned.

WOW!

Captain Redbeard's pet monkey is called Spinoza. This little rascal has been causing trouble since the very beginning of the LEGO Pirates theme.

Brick History

A group of Islanders, led by King Kahuka, appeared in six LEGO Pirates sets in 1994 and one 2001 set. They did battle with both the Pirates and the Imperial Soldiers to protect their island home.

Piece particulars

LEGO Pirates was the first LEGO theme to feature a musket, historical flintlock pistol, and cannons.

IT'S A SIGN!

Four different versions of the LEGO Pirates' Jolly Roger have appeared in more than 40 sets. In real life, the flag has been seen since as long ago as 1687.

LEGO® *STAR WARS*™ WORLDS

The LEGO® *Star Wars*™ theme
launched in 1999 to tie in with
the release of *Star Wars: Episode I
The Phantom Menace.* From the
beginning, the theme featured
sets based around the classic trilogy
of *Star Wars* films as well as the
prequels. To date, there have been more
than 475 LEGO *Star Wars* sets. There have
been sets based on all nine big-screen
movies, as well as three TV shows.
LEGO *Star Wars* is now the longest-running
licensed LEGO theme and will celebrate
its 20th anniversary in 2019.

PLENTY OF PLANETS

Miniature versions of
planets from the LEGO
Star Wars universe were
released in 2012 and 2013.
The series also
included a mini
Death Star and
an asteroid field.

Q What was the first
LEGO lightsaber duel?

A Lightsaber Duel (set 7101),
released in 1999, replicated
the fierce battle between
Qui-Gon Jinn and Darth
Maul on Tatooine.

WOW!

The planet of
Tatooine has the
most sets based
around it. There are
35 sets that have its
sandy surface as
their setting.

Brick History

Among the first
LEGO *Star Wars* sets
to be released in
1999 was the X-Wing
Fighter (set 7140).

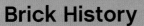

LOOK CLOSER

X-Wing Fighter (set 4502) from 2004
includes a version of Yoda's hut while
he is in hiding on Dagobah. A secret
compartment under Yoda's bed lets
him store his lightsaber safely.

AWESOME!

In 2012, LEGO minifigure paramedics stopped wearing white and suited up in bright red gear with reflective silver safety stripes.

REALLY?!

The slightly scary operating room in 2006's LEGO City Hospital (set 7892) includes a robot claw hand, a buzz saw, and a chain saw!

MEDICAL SCHOOL

The largest LEGO hospital is a special set for schools from 1993. The 522-piece LEGO Dacta Hospital (set 9364) has four beds, an operating theater, and a gym.

Piece particulars

Minifigure gurneys with hinged wheel pieces appeared in more than 30 sets between 1985 and 2011, when they were replaced by stretchers without wheels.

IT'S A SIGN!

Stickers in 1978's Hospital (set 231) include weighing scales, surgical gear, observation charts, and a chart for eye tests.

12

Windows in 1987's light-filled LEGO Town Emergency Treatment Center (set 6380)—but no door!

TOP 5

Air ambulances

1 **Red Cross Helicopter** (set 626), 1978

2 **Med-Star Rescue Plane** (set 6356), 1988

3 **Rescue Helicopter** (set 7903), 2006

4 **Helicopter Rescue** (set 4429), 2012

5 **Ambulance Plane** (set 60116), 2016

WE SHOULD SEE A DOCTOR ABOUT THIS!

Brick History

In 1975, the first LEGO Hospital (set 363) featured the forerunners to modern minifigures, including two who were built into the stretcher they were carrying!

PRICKLIEST PATIENT

Hedgehog from Mia's Vet Clinic (set 10728)

I STUDIED MEDICINE IN VEIN.

INJECTION MOLDING

The first LEGO medic to carry a hypodermic needle was the LEGO Minifigures Nurse in 2010. The small syringe is not sharp and has now appeared in more than 30 sets.

Piece particulars

The LEGO Minifigures Surgeon from 2012 has a unique printed piece that shows a LEGO skeleton figure torso. Perhaps it's an X-ray of 2016's Clumsy Guy minifigure!

FACT STACK

Minifigure medics debuted in Ambulance (set 606) and Red Cross Car (set 623) in 1978.

The first minifigure hospital was LEGO Town's Paramedic Unit (set 6364) in 1980.

Hospitals, ambulances, and doctors have appeared in LEGO® FABULAND and DUPLO sets.

GET WELL SOON

In the action-packed worlds of LEGO Town and LEGO City, it's good to know there's always a minifigure medic on call, and an ambulance is never far away!

BEHIND THE MASKS

Originally constructed from LEGO® Technic elements, the BIONICLE® theme features some of the LEGO Group's most exciting and complex storylines.

The BIONICLE Dictionary

Matoran: The most populous species in the BIONICLE universe. Each Matoran corresponds to an element but cannot control its power.

Toa: Heroes who protect the Matoran and the Great Spirit Mata Nui by using their elemental power to fight for good.

Turaga: Former Toa who gave up their powers to become "elders" and lead the Matoran.

Kanohi: Masks worn by the Matoran and Toa that give them power.

Makuta Teridax: The evil leader of the Brotherhood of Makuta, who put the Great Spirit into a coma and attempted to enslave the Matoran.

Q Are BIONICLE sets always made from LEGO Technic pieces?

A No. A special line using a mix of standard bricks and LEGO Technic elements was released between 2005 and 2007, totalling 12 sets. A new figure-building system was also introduced for sets after 2014.

Brick History

Early BIONICLE characters lived on the surface of the island of Mata Nui. In 2004, Toa Metru sets began to explore the hi-tech city of Metru Nui, deep beneath Mata Nui.

THE TOA

The first six full-sized BIONICLE heroes to be introduced in 2001 belonged to the Toa tribe. New versions of the six were released in 2015.

KOPAKA
Toa of Ice

GALI
Toa of Water

POHATU
Toa of Stone

TOP 5
Fearsome foes of the Toa

1 The spider-like **Visorak**.

2 **Bohrok:** swarming mecha-insects.

3 **Rahkshi:** living suits of armor.

4 **Umarak the Hunter:** a dark, ancient being.

5 The thieving and cruel **Piraka**.

AWESOME!

The six original Toa Mata were re-released in 2016, in a larger size with collectible golden masks.

Brick statistics

BIONICLE media

54 comics
Also collected as graphic novels

43 books
Including stories and guides

6 video games
Plus two mobile games

4 DVD movies
Starting with the *Mask of Light* in 2003

1 Netflix series
LEGO BIONICLE: *The Journey to One*

WOW!

The Battle of Metru Nui (set 8759) from 2005, is an 856-piece fortress playset—and the biggest set in the LEGO BIONICLE theme.

311

Number of LEGO BIONICLE sets released between 2001 and 2016.

REALLY?!

There are over 150 different Kanohi masks, which are worn by most beings in the BIONICLE universe.

ONUA
Toa of Earth

LEWA
Toa of Air

TAHU
Toa of Fire

HOME IS WHERE HEARTLAKE IS

Launched in 2012, LEGO® Friends was a big hit from day one. The theme follows the busy lives of five friends in and around their exciting hometown, Heartlake City.

FACT STACK

The five LEGO Friends stars are Stephanie, Olivia, Emma, Mia, and Andrea.

LEGO Friends was the first theme to use mini-dolls, which are larger and more realistic than minifigures.

More than 800 children and their families helped the LEGO Group get the theme just right.

To date, more than 150 LEGO Friends sets have been released.

Q What can you do at Heartlake City's Fun Park?

A There's a roller coaster, Ferris wheel, arcade, space ride, hot-dog van, and bumper cars! Five sets released in 2016 combine to create a world of amusements.

REALLY?!

Of all the LEGO Friends girls, busy bee Stephanie is in the most sets, appearing in more than 30. She does like to be involved in everything!

LOOK CLOSER

The departure board in Heartlake City Airport represents the home country of each designer working on the LEGO Friends team!

BILLUND 09:00
NEW YORK 10:30
BERLIN 11:15
MADRID 12:30
LONDON 15:00
PARIS 15:45
GLASGOW 17:10
PORTO 18:30
OSLO 20:45

CRUISING AROUND TOWN

There are all kinds of ways to get around Heartlake City! Here are some of the more unusual modes of transport.

Pop Star Tour Bus (set 41106)

Puppy Parade (set 41301)

Heartlake Hot Air Balloon (set 41097)

Dolphin Cruiser (set 41015)

AWESOME!

There are more than 200 different mini-dolls in the LEGO Friends world, including Alicia, Ben, Chloe, David, Ella, and James (pictured).

SCREEN STARS

LEGO Friends made its movie debut on Netflix and had its first direct-to-DVD movie in 2016.

TOP 5

Cutest LEGO Friends pets

1 Toffee the pug

2 Jazz the bunny

3 Maxie the cat

4 Fame the foal

5 Kiki the parrot

WOW!

In 2013, just a year after its release, LEGO Friends became a "core" theme, giving it a place among the LEGO greats, such as LEGO City and LEGO Space.

New colors were introduced to the LEGO palette in LEGO Friends sets: Dark Azur, Medium Azur, Aqua, Spring Yellow Green, Lavender, and Medium Lavender.

ENJOY YOUR STAY

Heartlake Grand Hotel (set 41101) is the biggest place in town! This 1,552-piece, three-story hotel is modular, meaning its rooms can be arranged in multiple ways.

BUILDING SIGHTS

Thanks to LEGO® Architecture and other advanced building themes, you can now enjoy the world's most impressive buildings from the comfort of your own home.

LET ME LIGHT YOUR WAY AROUND THESE FAMOUS SIGHTS.

33IN (84CM)

STATUE OF LIBERTY, USA

In 2000, a LEGO Sculptures set used 2,847 sand green pieces to depict a 33in (84cm) high Statue of Liberty (set 3450).

THE WHITE HOUSE, USA

The LEGO Architecture White House (set 21006) from 2010 uses a transparent minifigure head piece as the large lantern that hangs from the north portico of the official residence of the President of the United States.

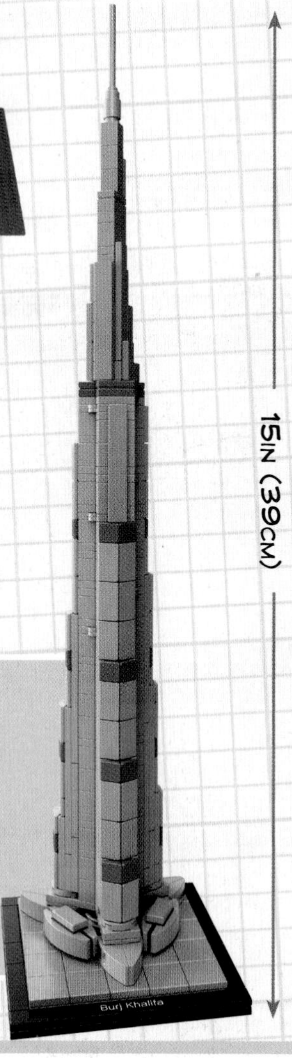

9IN (22CM)

15IN (39CM)

BURJ KHALIFA, UAE

Based on the world's tallest building, the 2016 Burj Khalifa (set 21031) is also the tallest set in the LEGO Architecture range, at more than 15in (39cm) high. It is the second LEGO set of this Dubai landmark.

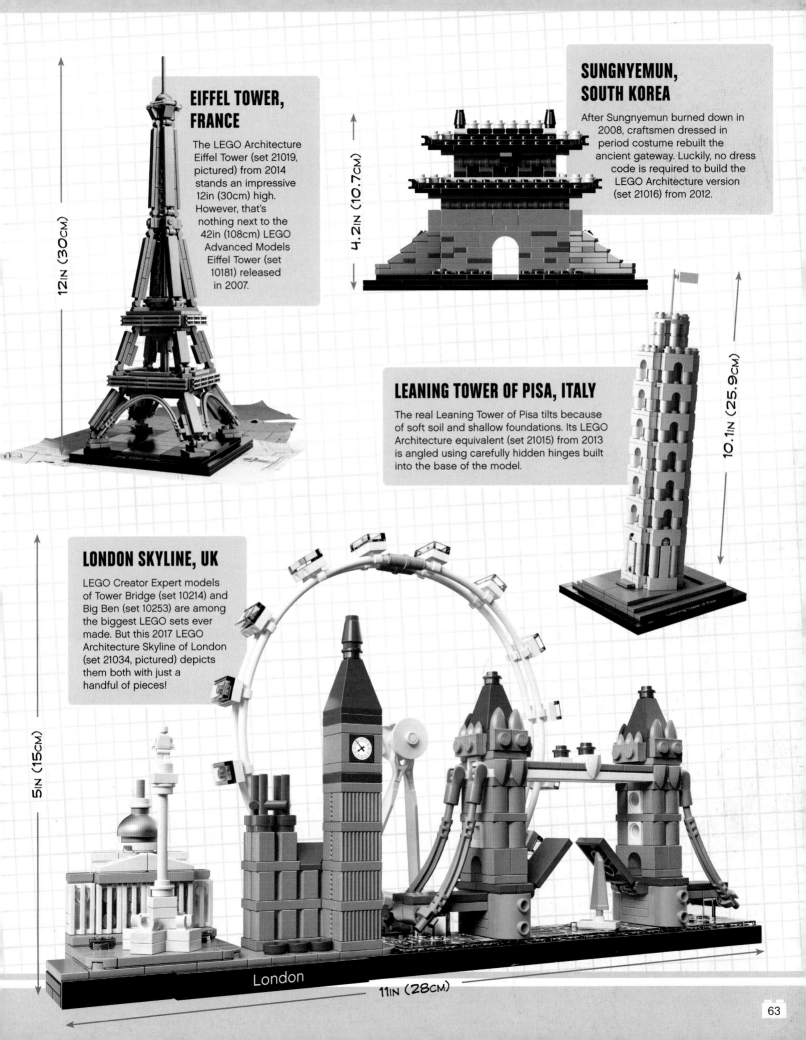

EIFFEL TOWER, FRANCE

The LEGO Architecture Eiffel Tower (set 21019, pictured) from 2014 stands an impressive 12in (30cm) high. However, that's nothing next to the 42in (108cm) LEGO Advanced Models Eiffel Tower (set 10181) released in 2007.

12in (30cm)

SUNGNYEMUN, SOUTH KOREA

After Sungnyemun burned down in 2008, craftsmen dressed in period costume rebuilt the ancient gateway. Luckily, no dress code is required to build the LEGO Architecture version (set 21016) from 2012.

4.2in (10.7cm)

LEANING TOWER OF PISA, ITALY

The real Leaning Tower of Pisa tilts because of soft soil and shallow foundations. Its LEGO Architecture equivalent (set 21015) from 2013 is angled using carefully hidden hinges built into the base of the model.

10.1in (25.9cm)

LONDON SKYLINE, UK

LEGO Creator Expert models of Tower Bridge (set 10214) and Big Ben (set 10253) are among the biggest LEGO sets ever made. But this 2017 LEGO Architecture Skyline of London (set 21034, pictured) depicts them both with just a handful of pieces!

5in (15cm)

London

11in (28cm)

Though the first LEGO flame piece wasn't introduced until 1993, LEGO fire service sets have been around since the 1950s and are still burning brightly today.

TOP 5

Burning builds

1 Abandoned building (set 60003)

2 Speedboat (set 60005)

3 Hot-dog stand (set 60110)

4 TV satellite tower (set 60111)

5 Lighthouse (set 60109)

NOW WHAT DID I COME UP HERE FOR?

AWESOME!

Three LEGO City Fire sets from 2016 feature stud-shooting hose pieces for firing "water" at the towering flames.

Q | Are all LEGO fire engines red?

A | No. Launch Evac 1 (set 6614) from LEGO Town's 1995 Launch Command subtheme is white, and 2006's LEGO City Airport Fire Truck (set 7891) is yellow.

IT'S A SIGN!

The LEGO Town Fire Department logo remained unchanged from 1978 to 2000. It was subtly updated for LEGO City in 2005, before being redesigned in 2012 (pictured).

Piece particulars

The transparent blue pieces that are used to show a spray of water are the same shape as the transparent orange pieces used to represent flames.

10

Number of LEGO fireboats that really float on water.

WHEEEEE!

POLE POSITION

The 2016 LEGO City Fire Station (set 60110) was the first to feature a new, corkscrew-style fire pole that minifigures can really slide down!

FIRE

2

TOP 5

LEGO coast-guard rescue stations

1 LEGOLAND Town Coastal Rescue Base (set 6387), 1989

2 LEGO Town Hurricane Harbor (set 6338), 1995

3 LEGO World City Coast Watch HQ (set 7047), 2003

4 LEGO City Coast Guard Platform (set 4210), 2008

5 LEGO City Coast Guard Head Quarters (set 60167), 2017

IT'S A SIGN!

The LEGO Town Coast Guard HQ (set 6435) from 1999 comes with red and green flags to show when it is safe to swim—and a printed sign to explain the system!

Brick History

In 1998, the LEGO Town Res-Q team provided coast-guard and other emergency response services in vehicles such as the Res-Q Cruiser (set 6473).

5

Different emblems have been emblazoned on LEGO coast-guard ships since 1991.

BE CAREFUL OUT THERE, BUDDY.

Piece particulars

Life got easier for the LEGO coast guard in 1990 with the invention of the first minifigure lifejacket. Ring-shaped lifebuoys followed in 1999.

AWESOME!

In 2013, the LEGO City coast guard got a new look, a new logo, and its first proper Coast Guard Plane (set 60015).

MOST DARING LAUNCH

Water Scooter, launched from Heavy Duty Rescue Helicopter (set 60166)

A TALE OF TWO COAST GUARDS

In 1976, Coast Guard Station (set 369) was released in Europe with yellow vehicles and featureless figures. In 1978, a near-identical set came out in the US—but now with white vehicles and some of the very first minifigures.

REALLY?!

LEGO City Coast Guard Patrol (set 60014) from 2013 features more grisly gray sharks than any other LEGO set.

HEY, I THOUGHT YOU WERE COMING TOO?

LOOK CLOSER

The LEGO Minifigures line got its first Lifeguard in 2010. Going by the initials on her swimsuit, she may just share a name with former LEGO Design Master Gitte Thorsen!

FACT STACK

Before LEGO Town got its own coast guard, it had 1985's Rescue-I Helicopter (set 6697).

C26 Sea Cutter (set 4022) from 1996 was the first coast-guard ship to really float on water.

A coast-guard station forms part of the 1996 LEGO Town set Wave Jump Racers (set 6334).

TO THE RESCUE

When LEGO Town and City minifigures stray too far from shore, the LEGO coast guard are ready to make a splash as they race to the scene.

HOME SWEET HOME

Who wouldn't want to live in a LEGO house? There's an endless range to choose from, and you never need to move when you can just rebuild!

FACT STACK

The LEGO Town Plan sets of the 1950s featured small homes built with about 20 bricks each.

In the 1960s and 1970s, sets such as House with Car (set 346) depicted realistic homes.

An Unexpected Gathering (set 79003) from 2012 recreates Bilbo Baggins' home from *The Hobbit*™.

The huge LEGO® *Simpsons*™ House (set 71006) from 2014 has seven rooms and a garage!

MOVING HOME

In 1973, the same stylish house was released as Swiss Villa (set 540) in the USA, Villa Mallorca in Denmark, and Italian Villa (set 356) in the rest of Europe.

REALLY?!

In some LEGO catalogs, Lionel Lion's Lodge (set 3678) from the 1982 FABULAND range was known as "The Story of the Noisy Neighbors!"

HAS ANYONE GOT ABOUT FIFTY EARPLUGS?

BRICK CHALLENGE

Look at your own home with LEGO builders' eyes and think about how you could recreate it with your collection of bricks.

AWESOME!

Livi's Pop Star House (set 41135) from the LEGO Friends theme comes with several rare printed pieces, including a gold disc and two sushi rolls.

TOP 5
LEGO Town vacation villas

1 Summer Cottage (set 6365), 1981

2 Holiday Home (set 6374), 1983

3 Weekend Home (set 6370), 1985

4 Vacation House (set 1472), 1987

5 Poolside Paradise (set 6416), 1992

AWESOME!

The LEGO® Monster Fighters Haunted House (set 10228) from 2012 has zombie heads built into the brickwork!

WOW!

Ole Kirk's House is where the LEGO Group began in 1932. In 2012, LEGO Group employees received a model of it (set 4000007) as a Christmas gift.

SWEETEST RETREAT

Gingerbread House (set 40139)

I'M THE HEAD OF THIS HOUSEHOLD!

LOOK CLOSER

A light brick in the fireplace of Winter Village Cottage (set 10229) fills the whole house with a warming glow throughout the winter months.

JOINED-UP THINKING

In 2007, the first LEGO Modular Buildings brought new levels of detail to a minifigure-scale world. Since then, this desirable neighborhood has kept on growing, as each new building slots seamlessly onto the last.

REALLY?!

Built into the details of Detective's Office (set 10246) from 2015 are all the clues you need to solve a cookie-smuggling mystery.

Q Is Market Street really a Modular Building?

A Though the fan-designed Market Street (set 10190) was released as part of the LEGO Factory theme, it was designed to fit the Modular format. Its status was confirmed when it was included in Mini Modulars (set 10230) in 2012.

Brick History

In 2012, Mini Modulars (set 10230) celebrated five years of the Modular Buildings range. The miniature street scene had 1,356 pieces and depicted every Modular Building released up to that point.

KEY DATES

2007
Café Corner (set 10182) and Market Street (set 10190, pictured)

2008
Green Grocer (set 10185)

2009
Fire Brigade (set 10197)

2010
Grand Emporium (set 10211)

LOOK CLOSER

An "out of order" launderette washing machine is actually a back way into the bank vault for a spot of literal money laundering in 2016's Brick Bank (set 10251).

1891

The build date commemorated on the Town Hall (set number 10224) is also the year that LEGO Group founder Ole Kirk Kristiansen was born.

Piece particulars

There is at least one white street lamp in every Modular Building to date. LEGO Set Designer Jamie Berard promised to keep using the piece to save it from being retired!

FACT STACK

Modular Buildings have stories that separate easily for access to the detailed interiors, like in Detective's Office (set 10246, pictured).

Each Modular Building can be quickly built on to any other using LEGO Technic pins.

LEGO Modular Buildings are the only modern sets to use the classic smiling minifigure face.

Since 2013, LEGO Modular Buildings have been part of the Creator Expert theme.

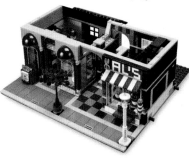

AWESOME!

The "sunburst" sign over the door of Café Corner (set 10182) is made by fanning out minifigure skis on a curving tube.

2011
Pet Shop
(set 10218)

2012
Town Hall
(set 10224)

2013
Palace Cinema
(set 10232)

2014
Parisian
Restaurant
(set 10243)

2015
Detective's
Office
(set 10246)

2016
Brick Bank
(set 10251)

2017
Assembly Square
(set 10255)

71

DIVE IN!

LEGO themes went into space and back in time before they ventured underwater. But when they finally took the plunge, these subaquatic worlds really made a splash!

WOW!

The 1997 LEGO Town set Deep Sea Bounty (set 6559) features a brick-built whale skeleton. Its tail is made from an airplane piece.

SUCKERS!

LEGO® Aquazone Hydronauts craft could pick things up using limpet-like suction-cups. These special pieces have never appeared in any other theme.

> DEEP, MAN.

12

Brand-new, brightly colored printed pieces were created for The Beatles' Yellow Submarine (set 21306).

TOP 5

LEGO® Atlantis deep-sea dwellers

1 Squid Warrior (set 8061)

2 Barracuda Guardian (set 7985)

3 Hammerhead Warrior (set 7984)

4 Lobster Guardian (set 7985)

5 Manta Warrior (set 8073)

IT'S A SIGN!

The LEGO® Aquazone Aquasharks styled their ships with scary stick-on eyes and teeth—plus a surprisingly smiley shark logo!

THIS PLACE IS A REAL DIVE.

KEY DATES

1995

The first LEGO Aquazone sets pitch brave, crystal-hunting Aquanauts against the Aquasharks in the first underwater LEGO theme.

1997

A new wave of Aquazone sets introduces the Aquaraiders—mineral hunters who are not afraid to smash up the seabed!

1998

Heroic Hank Hydro leads the Hydronauts into battle against the Stingrays in the third and final era of LEGO Aquazone.

2007

Almost sharing its name with an Aquazone faction, Aqua Raiders is a new theme in which treasure hunters tackle scary sea monsters!

2010

LEGO Atlantis explorers set out to find the fabled lost city of Atlantis, meeting many strange creatures along the way.

Q What is the biggest underwater-themed LEGO set?

A Portal of Atlantis (set 8078) from the LEGO Atlantis theme has 1,007 pieces, including two brick-built sharks and special treasure keys to unlock the portal!

Piece particulars

Crystal pieces were created especially for the LEGO Aquazone theme in 1995, and have since appeared in more than 150 sets.

REALLY?!

An unfortunate diver can be seen inside the squid in 2007's LEGO® Aqua Raiders Aquabase Invasion (set 7775). His skeleton still has its diving mask on!

73

SOMETHING OLD, SOMETHING NEW

The LEGO® NEXO KNIGHTS™ world is a place where advanced digital technology sits side-by-side with knights and monsters straight out of the medieval era.

Brick statistics

Jestro's Volcano Lair
(set 70323)

1,186 pieces
One of the biggest LEGO NEXO KNIGHTS sets

8 minifigures
Plus two Scurrier figures

6 NEXO Powers
Included on scannable shields

4 animals
Look out for a rat, chicken, spider, and frog

3 spell books
Including the scary Book of Monsters

Q How do you become a knight?

A Apprentices enroll at the Knights' Academy, a prestigious school where Merlok 2.0 teaches the next generation about combat, NEXO Powers, and the Knight's Code.

DO YOU LIKE THE NEW PLACE?

IT'S LAVA-LY!

NEXOgraphy of Knighton

The **Lava Lands** are a bleak volcanic wilderness full of dangerous monsters.

Knighton's capital city is called **Knightonia**, which is designed around the royal castle.

Diggington is a charming rural town in the northern Hill Country.

Auremville in the mountainous west is renowned for its riches.

AWESOME!

King Halbert's huge Knighton Castle (set 70357) swings open on hinges, just like many of the classic strongholds in the LEGO Castle theme.

BRICK CHALLENGE

Knight Lance grew up in a fancy Auremville mansion. Why not try building his home?

WOW!

NEXO KNIGHTS hero Clay comes from the village of Dnullib. Spelled backward that's Billund, home of the LEGO Group's headquarters.

Brick History

In 2017, new six-sided pieces offered the ability to combine three NEXO Powers on one shield and bring them to life in the NEXO KNIGHTS app.

100

Years of peace in Knighton before Jestro opened the Book of Monsters!

TOP 5

Mightiest NEXO Power shields

 1 **Cyclonic Strike** creates a giant, spinning fist that punches enemies.

 2 **Supersonic Shield** is an impenetrable green shield for the knights.

 3 **Formation of Fortitude** conjures up four battle-ready clones of whoever uses it.

 4 **Starfall** turns shooting stars into offensive mini-meteors.

 5 **Dreadful Disintegration** causes victims to start slowly disintegrating. Yuck!

WORLD CRAFTING

Combining virtual construction game *Minecraft* with real-world LEGO bricks was always going to build into something special. In 2013, the exciting LEGO® *Minecraft*™ theme was spawned!

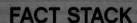

FACT STACK

LEGO *Minecraft* started out as an idea on the LEGO CUUSOO (now LEGO Ideas) website.

It took just 48 hours for LEGO *Minecraft* to win 10,000 votes from LEGO CUUSOO users!

LEGO *Minecraft* Micro World (set 21102) was released as a LEGO CUUSOO set in 2012.

A fully fledged theme called LEGO *Minecraft* followed Micro World into stores in 2013.

1,600

Pieces in the largest LEGO *Minecraft* set, The Village (set 21128), from 2016.

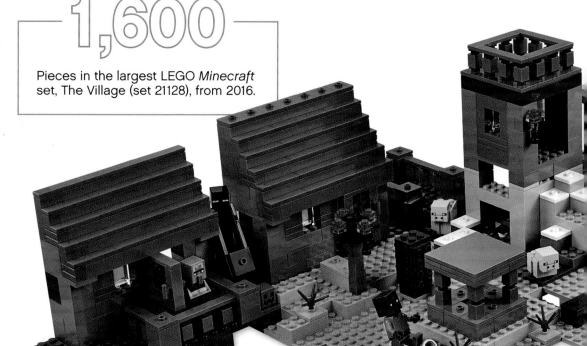

AWESOME!

The first four LEGO *Minecraft* sets came in cube-shaped boxes that looked like *Minecraft* building blocks.

OINK!

TOP 5
Buildable *Minecraft* Micro Mobs

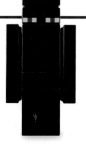

1 Steve (set 21102)

2 Creeper (set 21102)

3 Enderman (set 21107)

4 Zombie (set 21105)

5 Pig (set 21105)

BIGGEST BOSS

The Ender Dragon (set 21117)

Piece particulars

Minifigures in the LEGO *Minecraft* universe have unique cube-shaped heads that are 1.5 studs wide. These pieces have no studs on top, so their 2 studs-wide helmets clutch at the sides instead.

REALLY?!

Minecraft sets use so many 2x2 jumper plates that the LEGO Group had to make a new mold to keep up with demand.

WE ARE THE MOBS

"Mob" is the *Minecraft* name for any creature that is mobile. LEGO *Minecraft* features all six of the main Mob categories found in the game itself.

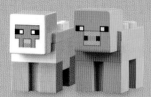

Sheep and Pigs are friendly **Passive Mobs**.

Cave Spiders are **Neutral Mobs** that attack if provoked.

Watch out for **Hostile Mobs**, such as Zombies and Skeletons.

You can befriend **Tameable Mobs**, such as Horses and Wolves.

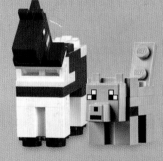

Utility Mobs, such as Iron Golems, can fight off Hostile Mobs.

Beware **Boss Mobs**, such as Withers, which are huge and very hostile!

LOOK CLOSER

Minecraft Mobs multiply by spawning. To see spawning in action, turn the round brick in The Dungeon (set 21119) and watch the baby Zombie move inside the cage-like spawner.

MICRO MANAGING

Each LEGO *Minecraft* Micro World set is made up of four modular sections that can be rearranged and mixed together to make a bigger *Minecraft* world.

A SET FOR

In the Chinese zodiac, 2017 is the Year of the Rooster. This little cockerel (set 40234) was released in time to mark the Chinese New Year on January 28, 2017.

No valentine could resist this brick-built Rose (set 852786). It's as fresh today as it was on its release in 2010.

Valentine's Day Dinner (set 40120) includes this gold-colored ring— or is it a bracelet?—for one lucky minifigure to wear.

A cuddly bunny with a bag of DUPLO bricks (set 852217) marked Easter in 2008. In 2016, a brick-built Easter Chick (set 40202) proved just as cute, if not so cuddly!

Fall Scene (set 40057) features tree trunks that can be decorated with autumnal colors. Any fallen leaves are swept up by minifigures!

This Halloween Bat (set 40090) is one of several LEGO sets released over the years to mark Halloween.

Several LEGO sets have marked US Thanksgiving, including a turkey (set 40011), a pilgrim (set 40204), and this turkey dressed as a pilgrim (set 40091)!

ALL SEASONS ● ● ● ● ● ● ● ● ● ● ● ● ● ● ●

MAY

The LEGO Group has marked *Star Wars* Day on May 4 with several exclusive sets, including Escape the Space Slug (set 6176782) in 2016.

JULY

US Flag (set 10042) from 2003 is one of two small stars-and-stripes builds released to mark US Independence Day, which is celebrated on July 4.

AUGUST

The LEGO Group's birthday is in August, and this slice of Birthday Cake (set 40048) helped it to celebrate in 2012.

DECEMBER

In 2009, the LEGO Holiday Countdown Candle (set 852741) was released. It features 24 numbered bricks—one to be removed each day in the lead-up to Christmas.

Since 2009, winter-themed Creator sets have combined to make a snow-capped village featuring a toy shop, bakery, market, train, and even Santa's Workshop (set 10245, pictured).

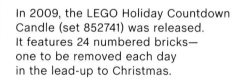

The first Christmas set was Santa and Sleigh (set 246) in 1977. Other brick-built Santas followed, including this Santa on Skis (set 1128) from 1999.

A TRIP TO MINILAND

From California to Malaysia, the heart of each and every LEGOLAND® park is its MINILAND, a remarkable LEGO brick recreation of landmarks from around the world.

Q Do the models in MINILAND move?

A Yes. Every year, the MINILAND vehicles at LEGOLAND Billund travel a distance equivalent to almost three trips around the world!

AWESOME!

Built at 1:50 scale, the Allianz Arena soccer stadium in LEGOLAND Deutschland features more than one million bricks and 30,000 minifigure spectators.

WORLD'S TALLEST LEGO BUILDING

Burj Khalifa at LEGOLAND Dubai, measuring 55ft (17m)

186

Miles (300km) of underground cable used to power MINILAND's moving parts at LEGOLAND Windsor.

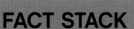

BRICK CHALLENGE

It takes around 40 bricks to build a MINILAND figure. Can you make a model of yourself in MINILAND scale?

FACT STACK

The first MINILAND was "Lilleby" (Little Town), at LEGOLAND Billund in 1968.

So far, more than 20 million LEGO bricks have been used to make MINILAND in Billund.

LEGO *Star Wars* scenes have formed part of the MINILAND world since 2011.

The MINILAND at LEGOLAND Dubai is inside a giant, see-through, air-conditioned dome.

TIPPING THE SCALE

Most MINILAND buildings are built at a scale between 1:20 and 1:40. In other words, they are between 20 and 40 times smaller than the real thing.

WOW!

In March 2017, a LEGO *Star Wars* Star Destroyer measuring 16ft (4.8m) was unveiled at MINILAND in LEGOLAND California.

LOOK CLOSER

A MINILAND ship at LEGOLAND Florida has the registry number 0937. Look at those numbers upside down and they spell out "LEGO."

A TRIP TO MINILAND

CONTINUED

1736

FANTASY FOREST

The LEGO® Elves theme launched in March 2015, with a TV special on the *Disney* Channel to introduce its magical characters and the forest world of Elvendale.

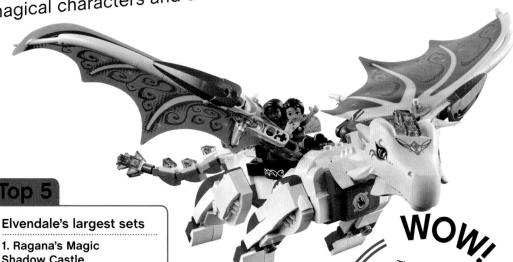

Top 5

Elvendale's largest sets

1. **Ragana's Magic Shadow Castle** (set 41180), 1,014 pieces

2. **Queen Dragon's Rescue** (set 41179), 833 pieces

3. **Skyra's Mysterious Sky Castle** (set 41078), 808 pieces

4. **Breakout from the Goblin King's Fortress** (set 41188), 695 pieces

5. **The Secret Market Place** (set 41176), 691 pieces

WOW!

The Dragons of Elvendale are linked to the elements water, fire, earth, and wind, just like the Elves. The Queen dragon, Elandra, uses a different one: love!

Piece particulars

The 1x4x2 ornamental fence piece was introduced in the LEGO Elves theme and has since popped up in other sets, including The *Disney* Castle (set 71040).

Ragana's Magic Shadow Castle

Queen Dragon's Rescue

Skyra's Mysterious Sky Castle

MAGICAL CREATURES

Elvendale is home to many enchanting animals, from owls and foxes to chameleons and pegasi.

Flamy the fox

Delphia the dolphin

Hidee the chameleon

Golden Glow the pegasus

Nascha the owl

Lil' Blu the baby bear

REALLY?!

In the LEGO *Elves* TV show, whenever fire elf Azari gets embarrassed, her ears turn white!

LOOK CLOSER

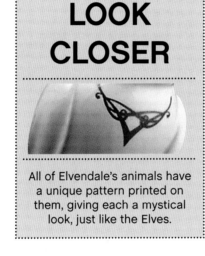

All of Elvendale's animals have a unique pattern printed on them, giving each a mystical look, just like the Elves.

Q | Is Elvendale a dangerous place?

A | It can be when the goblins are around! They use plant traps and catapults to make trouble for the elves.

YUM.

YUM!

 **AWESOME!** Each baby dragon hatches from a two-part dragon egg created especially for the LEGO Elves theme.

Breakout from the Goblin King's Fortress

The Secret Market Place

AT THE MOVIES

As well as making its own engrossing worlds, the LEGO Group has often teamed up with filmmakers to create play themes based on big-screen favorites.

THAT SIGN ISN'T VERY WELCOMING.

SHE'S BEHIND YOU. BOO!

LEGO® *GHOSTBUSTERS*™

Since 2014, there have been LEGO sets based on both the 1985 and 2016 *Ghostbusters* movies. With its 4,634 pieces, **LEGO *Ghostbusters* Firehouse Headquarters** (set 75827) was the largest LEGO set released in 2016.

LEGO® *HARRY POTTER*™

The longest running licensed theme after LEGO *Star Wars*, LEGO *Harry Potter* ran from 2001 to 2012, with a break in 2008–2009. Its dozens of sets included a detailed depiction of magical **Diagon Alley** (set 10217).

THIS IS ORC-WARD.

THIS IS NOT A WIZARD IDEA, SARUMAN.

LEGO® *THE LORD OF THE RINGS*™

LEGO *The Lord of the Rings* and LEGO *The Hobbit* launched in 2012, recreating Middle-earth in minifigure scale. The largest set from either theme was the 28in (73cm) tall **Tower of Orthanc** (set 10237).

CHAPTER THREE

CARS, PLANES, SHIPS, AND TRAINS

STREET CARS

There are more than 700 vehicles in LEGO® Town and LEGO City, of which these are just a few. Every one is the starting point for an endless number of adventures.

HEY YOU, STOP HORSING AROUND!

The Town **Horse Trailer** (set 6359) offers two modes of transport in one set.

1988 **Blizzard Blazer** (set 6524)

1986

1978

1982 **Mail Truck** (set 6651)

GO!

This open-top **Police Car** (set 621) is one of the first Town cars to hit the road.

POLICE

2009 Tractor (set 7634)

2010

This VIP stretch vehicle is part of **Helicopter and Limousine** (set 3222).

AG60102

IT'S USUALLY ME HOLDING UP THE TRAFFIC.

143 CITY

HA60026

2013

This eight-seater City bus stops off at **Town Square** (set 60026).

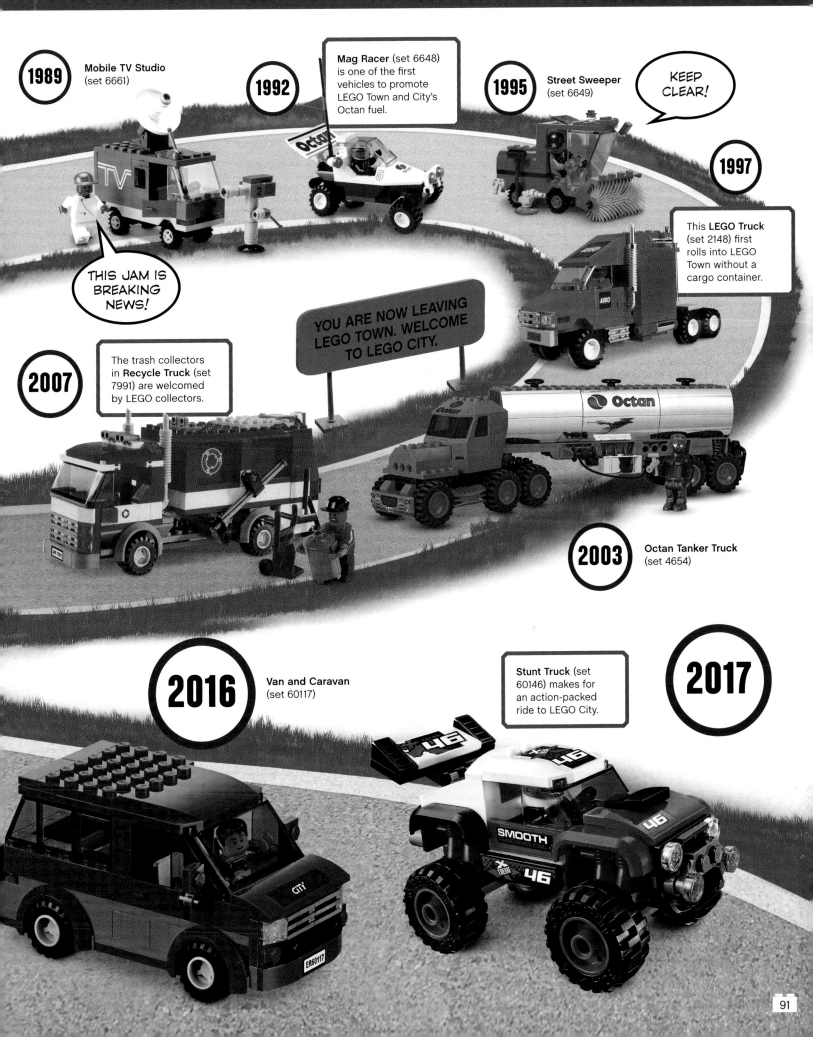

91

CAN YOU DIG IT?

LEGO fans love to build and rebuild, so it's no surprise that there are dozens of sets based on real-life construction and demolition vehicles!

FACT STACK

In 1964, the 64-piece Building Crane (set 804) was the first construction-themed vehicle.

Minifigure construction crews got to work in 1978, driving two diggers into LEGO Town.

There have been more than 40 construction-themed LEGO® Technic vehicles since 1979.

LEGO® DUPLO vehicles with a construction theme include the *Bob the Builder* range.

WOW!

The huge LEGO City Heavy Loader (set 7900) from 2006 carries an entire bridge that can be built into your LEGO City street system.

I GET PAID FOR DOZING ON THE JOB!

Piece particulars

The LEGO City Dozer (set 7685) from 2009 is one of only two sets to feature jet engine turbines but no jet engine housings.

LEGO CITY 5-12 7900

Brick History

In 2012, the LEGO City Mining subtheme featured several diggers and tippers. A special mining logo distinguishes these from similar construction vehicles.

IT'S A MINER DIFFERENCE!

21.6

Inches (55cm) is the full extent of the aptly named LEGO City XXL Mobile Crane (set 7249) from 2005.

LEGO CITY 7249

AWESOME!

The crane in 2010's LEGO City Level Crossing (set 7936) has two sets of wheels—one for roads and one for train tracks.

Brick statistics

28 diggers and loaders
In the LEGO Town and City themes

25 dumpers, tippers, and dozers
Across all of LEGO Town and City

7 mobile cranes and wreckers
In Town and City construction sets

3 cement mixers
1 in LEGO Town, 2 in LEGO City

1 Construct-o-Mech
Only in the world of THE LEGO® MOVIE™!

Q Are all LEGO construction vehicles yellow?

A Not all! There was a blue LEGO Town Tractor (set 6504) in 1988 and an orange digger in LEGO City Juniors Road Work Truck (set 10683) in 2015.

IT'S A SIGN!

The familiar symbol of a worker with a shovel has featured in many LEGO sets, and even got a "Minifigures at Work" makeover!

TOP 5

Building-site special pieces

1 Excavator scoop (1971)

2 Spring-loaded grabber (1974)

3 Tipper bucket (1974)

4 Cement mixer drum cone (1985)

5 Wrecking ball (2015)

BUILT FOR SPEED

If you've ever wanted to own a supercar, these LEGO racing sets can make your dreams come true. Many of them are based on real-life cars.

FACT STACK

The first LEGO racing set was Car with Trailer and Racer (set 650) in 1972.

The first minifigure racing driver came in the Race Car set (set 6609) in 1980.

More than 200 LEGO Racers sets came out from 2001 to 2013.

There have been three video games featuring LEGO racing cars.

REALLY?!

The LEGO Power Racers Tow Trasher (set 8140) from 2007 is designed to fall apart—purely for dramatic effect!

LOOK CLOSER

The Tiny Turbos subtheme of LEGO® Racers features fun, fast cars made with the fewest pieces possible. They are still packed with details, though—as the tiny stickered logos on this Rally Sprinter (set 8120) show!

REAL RACING

Since 2015, the LEGO® Speed Champions theme has recreated real-life racecars at minifigure scale, with impressively realistic results. Here are some of the sets released so far.

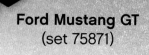

Ford Mustang GT
(set 75871)

Porsche 918 Spyder
(set 75910)

The wheels on LEGO Speed Champions cars have realistic interchangeable hubcaps, not seen in any other theme.

I AWESOME!

KEY DATES

1998

Radio Control Racer (set 5600) becomes the first radio-control LEGO vehicle. It comes with instructions for five different racecars.

2001

LEGO Racers sets screech into stores. They feature small cars with speed-demon driver pieces made especially for the theme.

2002

Racers step up a gear with larger sets, remote-control units, pullback motors, and drivers with minifigure heads on one-piece bodies.

2005

LEGO Power Racers mixes ramps, launchers, motors, fly-apart features, and spinning obstacles to create an array of exciting stunt vehicles.

2010

LEGO World Racers pitches minifigure team the X-treme Daredevils against the Backyard Blasters in racecars, race bikes, race boats, and race snowmobiles!

REALLY?!

The LEGO Racers Multi-Challenge Race Track (set 8364), released in 2003, comes with more than 10ft (3m) of speedway to race along.

YOU WON'T SEE ME FOR DUST!

WOW!

Each LEGO Speed Champions car comes with a unique minifigure dressed in accurate driver's gear for their team.

YOU'LL SEE ME ON THE PODIUM!

Mercedes-AMG GT3 (set 75877)

Audi R8 LMS Ultra (set 75873)

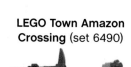

LEGO Town Amazon Crossing (set 6490)

GOING OFF-ROAD

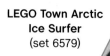

LEGO Town Arctic Ice Surfer (set 6579)

LEGO City Jungle Mobile Lab (set 60160)

LEGO Technic Arctic Rescue Unit (set 8660)

LEGO® Friends Jungle Bridge Rescue (set 41036)

LEGO City Arctic Outpost (set 60035)

ARCTIC-3

SNOW AND ICE

LEGO Town and City have had an Arctic outpost since 2000. Vehicles have adapted for the cold conditions, with strong wheels, sails, and skis to cope with slippery terrain.

FORESTS AND JUNGLE

Whether exploring the Amazon Jungle or the fictional forests of Heartlake City, these vehicles all have large, sturdy wheels—perfect for navigating dense foliage.

Not all LEGO vehicles are meant to stick to streets! For every cool city car, there's a mighty off-roader ready to tackle some tougher terrain.

LEGO® Creator Desert Racers
(set 31040)

BEACH AND DESERT

Heavy-tred tires get to grips with desert sand dunes on these four-wheel drive cars. The LEGO® Friends beach scooter has just three wheels, but still tackles sand with ease.

LEGO Technic Desert Racer
(set 42027)

LEGO City Volcano Crawler
(set 60122)

EVERY LIFEGUARD NEEDS A RESCUE PUG!

LEGO Friends Mia's Beach Scooter
(set 41306)

LEGO Model Team Big Foot 4x4
(set 5561)

LEGO City The Mine
(set 4204)

DIGGING THROUGH MINES? I KNOW THE DRILL.

ROCKS AND MOUNTAINS

Equipped with drills and jackhammers, these specialist LEGO vehicles are ready for a bumpy ride over rocks, in mines, or on red-hot lava.

In the battle between LEGO® DC Comics Super Heroes and their criminal counterparts, victory depends on what vehicle you drive! Here are some of the best and the baddest.

Wonder Woman's Invisible Jet is made using almost all transparent pieces.

THE CONTROLS ARE HARD TO READ.

AWESOME!

IT'S A SIGN!

The symbol on Green Lantern's spaceship (set 76025) is shaped like a green lamp: the insignia of intergalactic peacekeeping group the Green Lantern Corps.

FACTS STACKED

The first LEGO DC Universe Super Heroes sets came out in 2012.

In 2014, the theme became LEGO DC Comics Super Heroes.

Heroes in the theme can call on almost 40 different modes of transport.

Bad guys are at the controls of more than 20 different vehicles.

TOP 5

Mighty micros sets

1 **Catwoman's** Catmobile has ears and a tail!

2 **The Flash** drives a lightning-fast red racer.

3 **Killer Moth's** car gets ahead by a nose!

4 **Superman's** supercar flies along with outstretched arms.

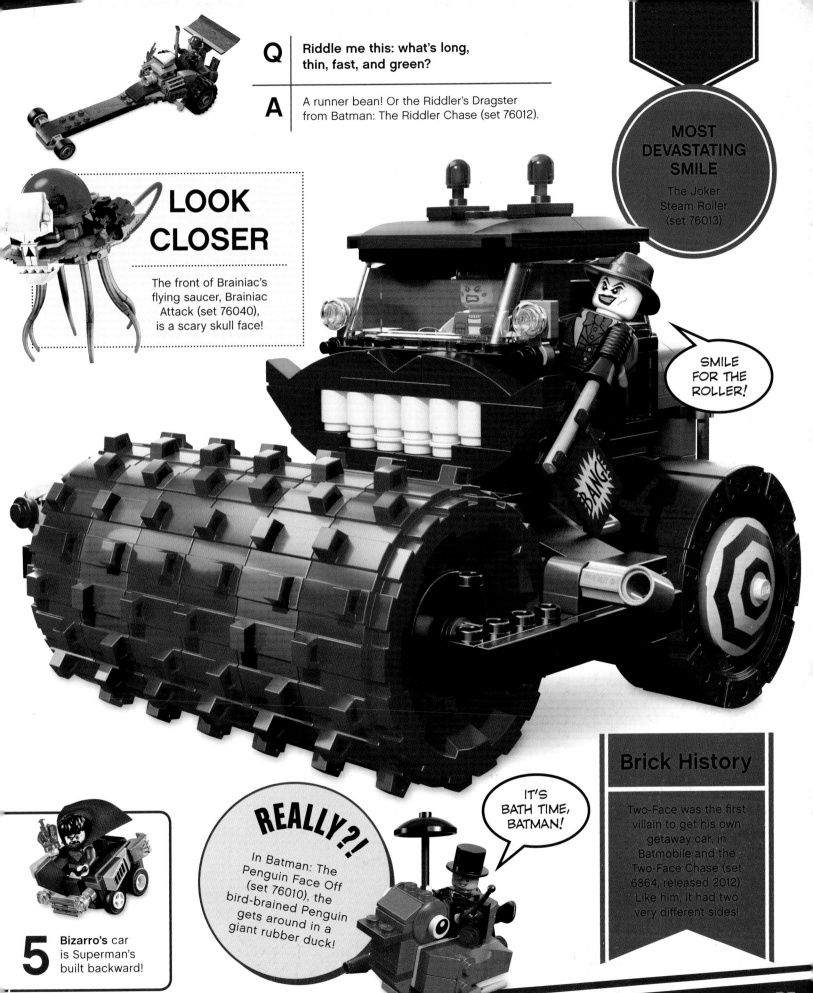

Q Riddle me this: what's long, thin, fast, and green?

A A runner bean! Or the Riddler's Dragster from Batman: The Riddler Chase (set 76012).

LOOK CLOSER

The front of Brainiac's flying saucer, Brainiac Attack (set 76040), is a scary skull face!

MOST DEVASTATING SMILE

The Joker Steam Roller (set 76013)

SMILE FOR THE ROLLER!

Brick History

Two-Face was the first villain to get his own getaway car, in Batmobile and the Two-Face Chase (set 6864, released 2012). Like him, it had two very different sides!

IT'S BATH TIME, BATMAN!

REALLY?!

In Batman: The Penguin Face Off (set 76010), the bird-brained Penguin gets around in a giant rubber duck!

5 Bizarro's car is Superman's built backward!

BAT-VEHICLES

With a Batcave full of crime-fighting cars and other hi-tech transport, Batman is always on the move in the LEGO® Batman and LEGO DC Super Heroes themes.

FACT STACK

The first LEGO Bat-vehicles hit the streets in 2006, in the LEGO Batman theme.

In 2012, LEGO Batman became part of the DC Super Heroes theme.

To date, there have been more than 40 LEGO Bat-vehicles.

There are 10 different LEGO Batmobiles, all of them black!

TOP 5
Batmobiles

1 The first Batmobile from **2006** has a massive missile in the hood.

2 This **2014** Batmobile looks like a Formula 1 racing car.

3 The Batmobile from **2015** has a classic 1930s hot rod vibe.

4 Released in **2016**, this Batmobile is straight out of the 1960s!

5 This **2016** Batmobile is compact but heavily armored.

AWESOME!

There have been two LEGO Bat-Tanks. The latest (in set 76055) has a front section that folds upright to make a huge battering ram!

Brick statistics

5 Batwings
Plus a backpack glider

5 Batcycles
Including one with a sidecar

5 Batcopters
Including Mighty Micros

3 Batboats
Plus a jetski and a scuba vehicle

2 Batman buggies
Ideal for the desert or the beach

1 Batman dragster
It's a looong story...

15
Points of articulation on the giant Bat-Mech.

DID THAT 'COPTER NOT GET THE MEMO?

I THOUGHT I'D BRIGHTEN UP THIS PAGE.

MOST COLORFUL BAT-VEHICLE

Mighty Micros Batcopter (set 76069)

Q | Is the Tumbler a Batmobile?

A | Batman used the Tumbler (set 7888) as his main mode of transport for a while and it has, on occasion, been referred to as one of his Batmobiles.

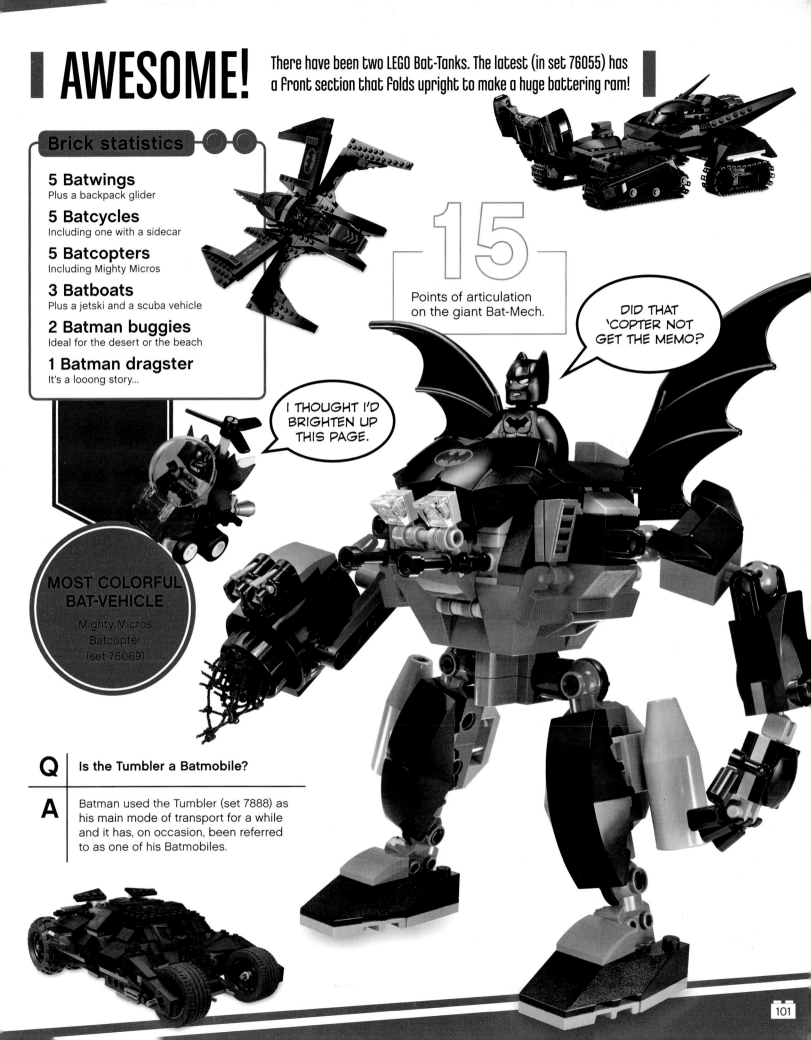

Famous four-wheelers from film and TV

1   **The Patty Wagon.**
Of all the zany vehicles in the
LEGO® *Spongebob Squarepants*™
theme, this burger on wheels from
Krusty Krab Adventures (set 3833)
has to be the craziest.

2   **The Mystery Machine (set 75902).**
This *Scooby-Doo* van has space for
mystery-solving tools including a
camera, noticeboards, computers—
and a giant sandwich for Shaggy
and Scooby to share!

3   **Ecto-1 (set 75828).**
This set from the 2016 movie
Ghostbusters has room inside
for all four ghoul-catching heroes.
It is based on a 1980 Cadillac
Hearse Wagon.

CARS

4 **The DeLorean Time Machine (set 21103).** This time-traveling car comes with instructions to turn it into the three versions seen in all three *Back to the Future* movies.

5 **The Simpsons' family car.** This car from *The Simpsons* has a large sunroof to make room for Marge Simpson's hair! It fits in the garage of The Simpson's House (set 71006).

6 **The Weasley's Ford Anglia.** The Weasley's flying family car appeared in two LEGO® *Harry Potter*™ sets: Escape from Privet Drive (set 4728) and Hogwarts Express (set 4841).

BIG AND BOLD

Some of the biggest LEGO vehicles look like they should be built for display rather than play purposes, but these impressive models all offer hours of building fun and plenty of interactive detail.

In the 1970s, LEGO® Hobby Set vehicles were among the first designed for play *and* display.

The LEGO® Model Team range was the home of large-scale vehicles in the 1980s and 1990s.

Today, the most challenging vehicles to build are part of the LEGO® Creator Expert theme.

LARGE-SCALE RAIL
Part of the 1970s Hobby Set range, Thatcher Perkins Locomotive (set 396) is the only LEGO train engine larger than minifigure (or DUPLO figure) scale.

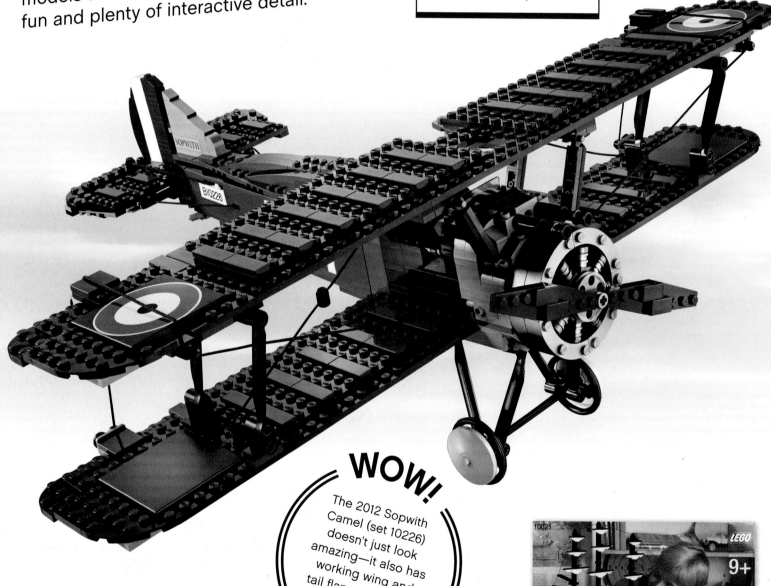

WOW!
The 2012 Sopwith Camel (set 10226) doesn't just look amazing—it also has working wing and tail flaps, controlled by a joystick in the cockpit.

▌AWESOME!
The 1978 model ship *USS Constellation* (set 398) is so fondly remembered that it was re-released in 2003 (set 10021), complete with retro packaging.

A surf scene in the homely interior of Volkswagen T1 Camper Van (set 10220) includes the initials of the set's designer, John-Henry Harris!

Brick History

In 2003, Wright Flyer (set 10124) was released to mark the 100th anniversary of the first real-world powered airplane. It has 670 pieces in just five colors.

Piece particulars

The car door handles on the MINI Cooper (set 10242) from 2014 are more usually used as minifigure ice skates!

27

Inches (69cm)—the wingspan of the Boeing 787 Dreamliner (set 10177), the largest of any LEGO aircraft.

REALLY?!

The biggest set in the advanced LEGO Model Team range, Giant Truck (set 5571) has 1,757 pieces—including a cat for a hood ornament!

TIR

MT 5571

STEPPING UP A GEAR

As well as looking incredible, the biggest LEGO Technic vehicles are marvels of miniature engineering—and they keep on getting bigger with each passing year! Here are the biggest LEGO Technic vehicles ever.

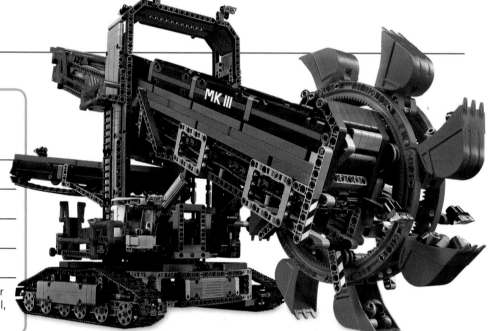

1

3,929 PIECES
BUCKET WHEEL EXCAVATOR

SET NUMBER	42055
YEAR RELEASED	2016
HEIGHT	16in (41cm)
LENGTH	28in (72cm)
FUNCTIONS	Motorized caterpillar tracks, bucket wheel, and conveyor belts.

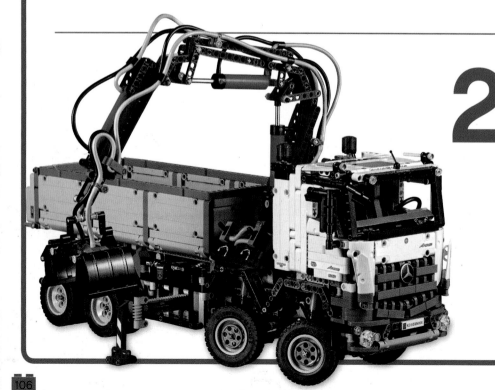

2

2,793 PIECES
MERCEDES-BENZ AROCS 3245

SET NUMBER	42043
YEAR RELEASED	2015
HEIGHT	22in (57cm) max.
LENGTH	29in (75cm)
FUNCTIONS	Motorized outriggers, crane arm, grabber, and tipper body.

3

2,704 PIECES
PORSCHE 911 GT3 RS

SET NUMBER	42056
YEAR RELEASED	2016
HEIGHT	6in (17cm)
LENGTH	22in (57cm)
FUNCTIONS	Working gearbox and steering, suspension, and adjustable spoiler.

5

2,048 PIECES
MERCEDES-BENZ UNIMOG U 400

SET NUMBER	8110
YEAR RELEASED	2011
HEIGHT	12in (30cm)
LENGTH	19in (48cm)
FUNCTIONS	Motorized winch and pneumatic crane with working grabber.

4

2,606 PIECES
MOBILE CRANE MK II

SET NUMBER	42009
YEAR RELEASED	2013
HEIGHT	30in (77cm) max.
LENGTH	23in (59cm)
FUNCTIONS	Motorized outriggers, extendable crane arm, and winch.

STATION TO STATION

LEGO passenger trains have been getting LEGO citizens to where they need to go since... before there were LEGO citizens! Some are superfast, while others belong to the age of steam.

Brick History

In 1976, Western Train (set 726) was the first to carry passengers, in the form of three cowboy figures and a brick-built horse.

IT'S A SIGN!

In the 1980s, most LEGO trains came with sticker sheets featuring the logos of different national rail operators, so you could customize your train according to your country!

WOW!

Designed for use with the 1991 Metroliner (set 4558), Club Car (set 4547) from 1993 is the only double-decker LEGO Trains set.

HI! DO YOU LIKE MY SHIRT?

TOP 5
First-class train travelers

1 **Classic Space Fan** aboard Holiday Train (set 10173), 2006.

2 **Journalist** from High-Speed Passenger Train (set 60051), 2014.

3 **High-Roller** on the Metroliner (set 4558), 1991.

4 **Tourist** from Passenger Train (set 7938), 2010.

AWESOME!

The LEGOLAND® Train (set 4000014) is a very rare replica of a ride at LEGOLAND Billund. It was given away to a few lucky fans in 2014.

The LEGOLAND® Train

LEGO
Ages 10+
4000014
548 pcs
Building Toy

No. B / 80

DREAM DESIGNS

When 2009's awesome Emerald Night (set 10194) was being designed, the LEGO Group flew 10 fan builders to its head office in Denmark, then got them to describe their dream LEGO train.

REALLY?!

Passengers could drive their cars onto 1999's futuristic Railway Express (set 4561) before heading to the onboard pizza restaurant!

Piece particulars

The large gray switches that controlled 12-volt trains in the 1980s could also remotely operate lights, signals, points, level crossings, and even wagon separation.

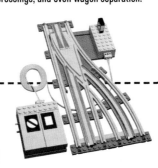

IT'S WHY I'M WEARING SHADES.

5 Definitely Not a Spy on the High-Speed Train (set 4511), 2003.

7 Speeds to choose from with 2014's superfast High-Speed Passenger Train (set 60051).

KEY DATES

1966
The first powered LEGO train features a 4.5-volt battery pack and special train wheels, and runs on new blue track pieces.

1969
Mains-powered LEGO trains driven by a 12-volt conductor rail and the first powered rail-switching points are introduced in Europe.

1980
A new look for LEGO Trains includes realistic gray tracks and a revamped 12-volt system offering a wealth of remote-control functions.

1991
A single 9-volt mains-powered system replaces both 4.5-volt battery power and 12-volt mains power as the standard for LEGO Trains.

2006
The LEGO Trains theme is integrated into LEGO City, and a new infrared remote-control system powered by rechargeable batteries is launched.

2010
The first of several LEGO City trains designed specifically for use with a battery-operated LEGO Power Functions motor is released.

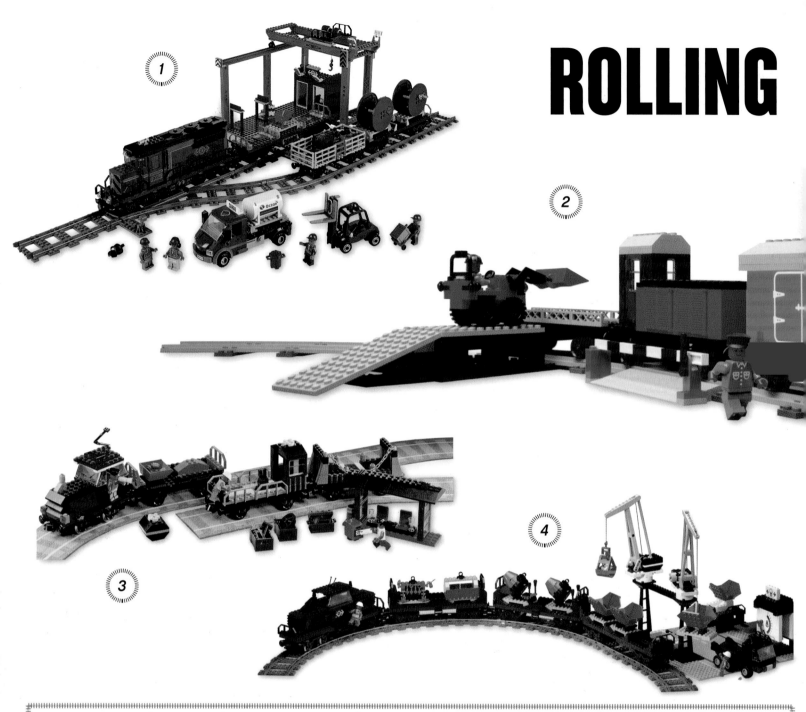

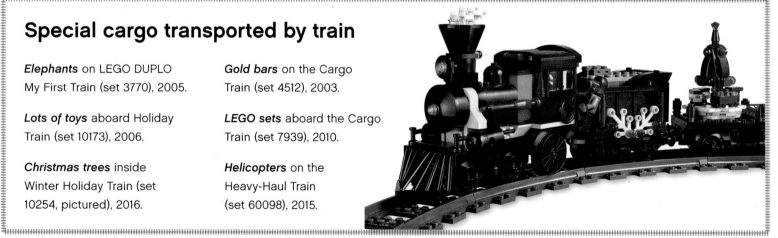

Special cargo transported by train

Elephants on LEGO DUPLO
My First Train (set 3770), 2005.

Lots of toys aboard Holiday
Train (set 10173), 2006.

Christmas trees inside
Winter Holiday Train (set
10254, pictured), 2016.

Gold bars on the Cargo
Train (set 4512), 2003.

LEGO sets aboard the Cargo
Train (set 7939), 2010.

Helicopters on the
Heavy-Haul Train
(set 60098), 2015.

STOCK

Classic cargo trains

1   *Cargo Train (set 60052)*, from 2014 has a spacious cattle truck, plus room for a fuel tank, a forklift, and two giant cable drums!

2   *Diesel Freight Train Set (set 7720)*, from 1980 carries cargo loaded onto it by a digger—as well as the digger itself!

3   *Classic Train (set 3225)*, from 1998 has a fragile crate of glasses amid its cargo, and a $100 note hidden among the mail!

4   *Freight and Crane Railway (set 4565)*, from 1996 comes with a working scale for weighing cargo that includes two cement mixers!

5   *Cargo Train Deluxe (set 7898)*, from 2006 has an onboard crane for lifting engines, oil drums, and even sports cars on its flatbed wagons!

6   *Maersk Train (set 10219).* This 1,237-piece train from 2011 is loaded with three huge cargo containers, including one refrigerator container.

SET SAIL!

There are enough LEGO boats and ships to fill an ocean—well, at least a couple of bathtubs! Some of them float, while others are designed to look sunken.

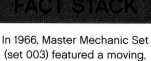
2,741

Number of pieces in the biggest LEGO ship: MetalBeard's Sea Cow (set 70810) from THE LEGO® MOVIE™.

The 2015 LEGO City Deep Sea Exploration Vessel (set 60095) comes with a shipwreck that collapses when you pull a hidden lever!

REALLY?!

Some LEGO vessels can float using special watertight hull pieces. The first was Tugboat (set 310), released in 1973.

WOW!

In 2005, two LEGO® Vikings sets featured longboats coming under attack from a dragon and a giant sea serpent!

Q When was the first LEGO Pirates ship launched?

A Black Seas Barracuda (set 6285) first set sail in 1989. It made such a splash that it was re-released as a LEGO Legends set (set 10040) in 2002.

AWESOME!

OCEANS APART

The LEGO Technic Ocean Explorer (set 42064) from 2017 has a whopping 1,327 pieces. The LEGO Creator Ocean Explorer (set 31045) from 2016 packs all its details into just 213!

TOP 5

Fanta-sea ships

1 LEGO Castle Troll Warship (set 7048)

2 LEGO® Legends of Chima™ Cragger's Command Ship (set 70006)

3 LEGO Elves Naida's Epic Adventure Ship (set 41073)

4 LEGO Ultra Agents Ocean HQ (set 70173)

5 LEGO® NINJAGO® *Destiny's Shadow* (set 70623)

Piece particulars

The LEGO KNIGHTS KINGDOM Rogue Knight Battleship (set 8821) from 2006 is the only set to use dragon wing pieces as ship's sails!

WOW!

The LEGO City Speedboat (set 7244) from 2005 doesn't just float on water—it zooms along it using a battery-powered motor!

Brick History

In 2016, LEGO® Education released a 1,184-piece working model of The Panama Canal (set 2000451), with four adjustable locks and five model ships.

UP, UP, AND AWAY

These amazing airplanes and high-flying helicopters are packed so full of play features, it's a wonder they ever get off the ground!

PLANE PACKAGING

LEGO® DUPLO® Airplane (set 5504) was released in 2005. It comprises 30 standard DUPLO bricks stored within a special airplane-shaped container.

LEGO Coast Guard Station 575

Brick History

The historic first flight by a minifigure was made by the helicopter pilot in the Coast Guard Station (set 575), a US-only set from 1978.

LOOK CLOSER

The goods being transported by plane in 2013's Cargo Terminal (set 60022) include two brick-sized LEGO sets—including the LEGO City Cement Mixer (set 60018) from the same year!

Q Why is there a set with a spaceship on top of a plane?

A Until 2012, real-world jumbo jets were used to transport space shuttles in the US. This was the inspiration for the 1995 LEGO Town set Shuttle Transcon 2 (set 6544).

TOP 5
Heavy-duty helicopters

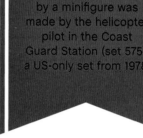

1 Light & Sound Rescue Helicopter (set 6482)

2 Fire Helicopter (set 7206)

3 T-rex Hunter (set 5886)

4 Arctic Helicrane (set 60034)

5 Volcano Heavy-Lift Helicopter (set 60125)

The first LEGO aircraft was the 79-piece Aeroplanes (set 311), which flew into stores in 1961.

More than 100 LEGO Town sets and 80 LEGO City sets feature planes or helicopters.

The biggest LEGO aircraft is the LEGO Technic Cargo Plane (set 42025) from 2014.

There were two planes in the LEGO® FABULAND theme. Both of them were flown by birds!

WOW!

The biplane in the LEGO City Airport Air Show (set 60103) from 2016 has a platform on top for a daredevil wing-walker!

I WISH I'D GONE BUSINESS CLASS.

REALLY?!

One of the strangest LEGO City planes is Cargo Heliplane (set 60021) from 2013. As its name suggests, it is half helicopter, half airplane.

5

Pieces used to make each airplane in 2014's Billund Airport (set 4000016).

SKY-HIGH SALES

Several aircraft sets have been made specially for sale on airlines. Holiday Jet (set 4032) from 2003 came with different logo decorations depending on which airline you were traveling with.

LC 7893

IT'S A SIGN!

In a change from the airline logos of LEGO Town, LEGO City Airlines uses a stylized bird as its logo.

Piece particulars

The 54-stud-wide wing plate first used in Passenger Plane (set 7893) from 2006 is one of the largest LEGO pieces ever produced!

MY BUSINESS IS REALLY TAKING OFF!

1

2

3

4

5

High-flying vehicles from across the LEGO world

1   Creative Ambush (set 70812). This 2014 airplane from THE LEGO® MOVIE™ started out as a kebab stand—but was rebuilt in the battle against Lord Business!

2   Witch's Windship (set 6037). She may have a broomstick, but this LEGO Castle minifigure witch prefers to fly using dragon power in this 1997 set!

3   King Crominus' Rescue (set 70227). Cragger's Fire Helicroctor comes from a LEGO Legends of Chima set released in 2015. It's ideal if you need to be somewhere in a snap!

4   Aaron Fox's Aero-Striker V2 (set 70320). Battling Ash Attackers in the LEGO® NEXO KNIGHTS™ world, this crossbow-shaped set shot into being in 2016.

5   Flying Time Vessel (set 6493). Part pirate ship, part airplane, and possibly even part dragon, the LEGO® Time Cruisers' craft would look strange in any era, but was released in 1996.

6   Expedition Balloon (set 5956). This LEGO® Adventurers vessel, from 1999, is the only set to ever feature this immense airship piece.

THE LIMIT

6

THE TRAFFIC UP HERE IS TERRIBLE.

8

7

7 **Aira's Pegasus Sleigh (set 41077).**
Pulled by silver-winged steeds
Starshine and Rufus, this 2015 set
takes LEGO® Elves Aira and Azari
on an airborne adventure.

8 **Aero Nomad (set 7415).**
Brave LEGO Adventurers use
this hot-air balloon to make
their way up Mount Everest
in this 2003 set.

NINJA, GO!

Q What is the biggest LEGO NINJAGO vehicle set?

A Final Flight of Destiny's Bounty (set 70738) has 1,253 pieces. The flying ship in the set measures 23in (59cm) long.

Ninja skills can only get you so far. The ninja need some fast vehicles to get around the vast world of NINJAGO sets in—and so do their enemies!

REALLY?!

Instead of serving snacks, the possessed street-food cart in Master Wu Dragon (70734) fires spooky ghost disks at the ninja.

Piece particulars

The Raid Zeppelin (set 70603) is the only LEGO set that contains curved and tapered panel pieces in dark orange.

NINJA, FLY!

Airjitzu is a fighting style that allows the ninja to fly. Ninja minifigures can take to the sky in Airjitzu Flyers—spinning capsules that are launched using a rip cord.

TOP 5
Enemy vehicle weapons

1 The mech arms on the **Destructoid** (set 70726).

2 The whipping tail on the **Anacondrai Crusher** (set 70745).

3 The cannons on **Misfortune's Keep** (set 70605).

4 The spinning saw on the **Hover Hunter** (set 70720).

5 The spiked wheels on the **Chain Cycle Ambush** (set 70730).

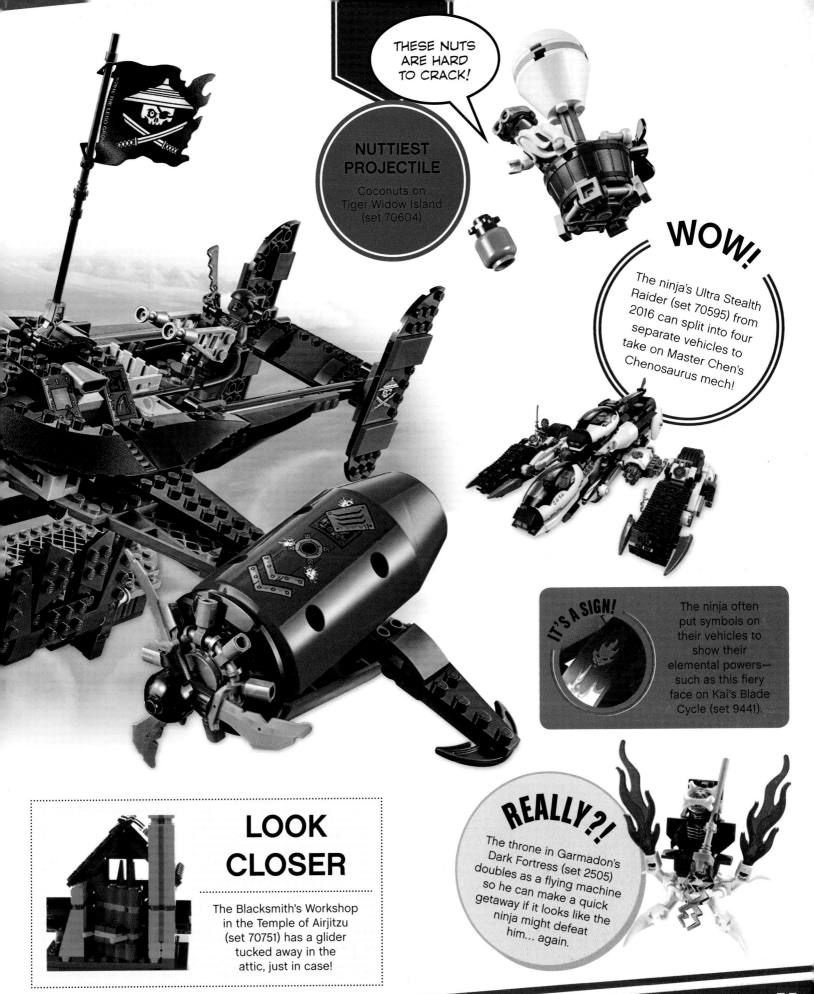

THESE NUTS ARE HARD TO CRACK!

NUTTIEST PROJECTILE

Coconuts on Tiger Widow Island (set 70604)

WOW!

The ninja's Ultra Stealth Raider (set 70595) from 2016 can split into four separate vehicles to take on Master Chen's Chenosaurus mech!

IT'S A SIGN!

The ninja often put symbols on their vehicles to show their elemental powers—such as this fiery face on Kai's Blade Cycle (set 9441).

LOOK CLOSER

The Blacksmith's Workshop in the Temple of Airjitzu (set 70751) has a glider tucked away in the attic, just in case!

REALLY?!

The throne in Garmadon's Dark Fortress (set 2505) doubles as a flying machine so he can make a quick getaway if it looks like the ninja might defeat him... again.

BIG STEPS FOR MECHS

Mechs have walked the LEGO world for many years. Mechanical suits manned by minifigures, these innovative machines are always receiving upgrades and getting bigger with every step.

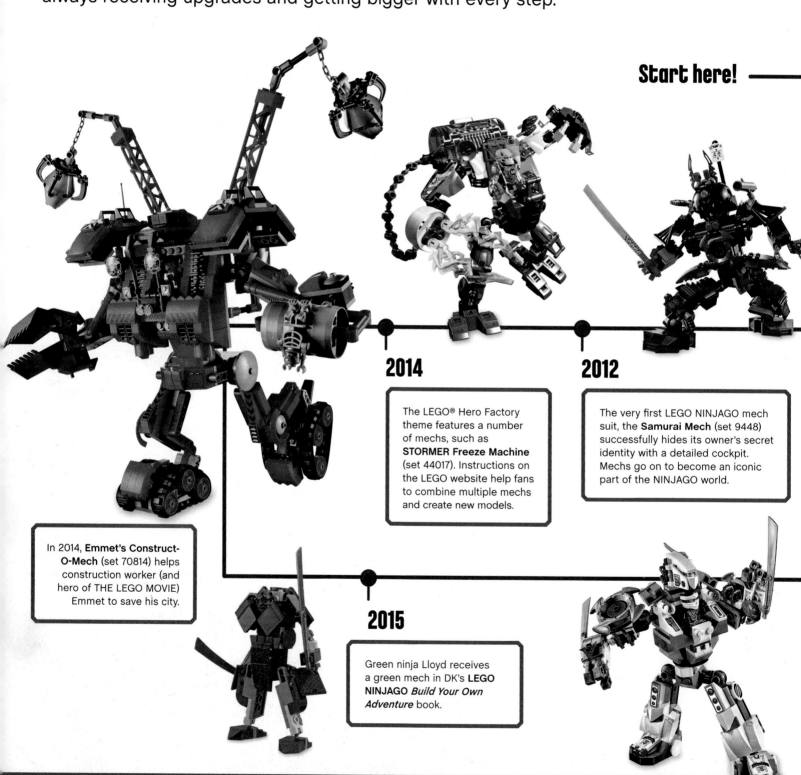

Start here!

2014

The LEGO® Hero Factory theme features a number of mechs, such as **STORMER Freeze Machine** (set 44017). Instructions on the LEGO website help fans to combine multiple mechs and create new models.

2012

The very first LEGO NINJAGO mech suit, the **Samurai Mech** (set 9448) successfully hides its owner's secret identity with a detailed cockpit. Mechs go on to become an iconic part of the NINJAGO world.

In 2014, **Emmet's Construct-O-Mech** (set 70814) helps construction worker (and hero of THE LEGO MOVIE) Emmet to save his city.

2015

Green ninja Lloyd receives a green mech in DK's **LEGO NINJAGO** *Build Your Own Adventure* book.

One of the first LEGO mechs, the LEGO Space Futuron **Strategic Pursuer** (set 6848) allows its solo pilot to safely carry out scientific research on distant planets.

1988

2001

When LEGO Space explorers discover life on Mars, they also discover menacing-looking Martian technology, such as the **Recon Mech RP** (set 7314).

2006

Inspired by hi-tech mechs in Japanese manga, the LEGO® Exo-Force theme centers around mighty mech battles. The **Grand Titan** (set 7701) stands over 7.5in (19cm) tall.

Mechs submerge to walk the seafloor in LEGO Atlantis sets in 2010. The **Undersea Explorer** (set 8080) transforms from a multi-wheeled rover into this well-defended mech with torpedo launcher.

2010

The **Magma Mech** (set 8189) is kitted out with everything the LEGO® Power Miners need to fight dangerous Lava Monsters, including a spiraled drill piece and grabbing claw.

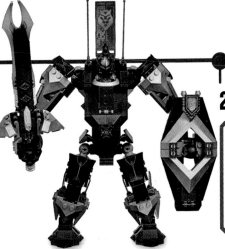

Ice ninja Zane gets his first mech just in time to take on the Ghost Army in **Titan Mech Battle** (set 70737). The four-armed Ghost Mech-enstein (left) is slightly taller than Zane's Titan Mech (far left).

2016

LEGO NEXO KNIGHTS theme's resident inventor, Robin, builds himself **The Black Knight Mech** (set 70326). This mech measures over 12in (31cm) tall from flag to foot.

WOW!

Clay's Rumble Blade (set 70315) is half car, half sword: the perfect vehicle for bringing speed to sword-fighting!

When it comes to protecting their homeland from a villain named Jestro and his monsters, a sword and shield aren't always enough. Both the NEXO KNIGHTS team and their enemies have fleets of vehicles.

Piece particulars

The NEXO KNIGHTS theme introduced a new pointed windshield piece, which features on many of the theme's vehicles.

IT'S A SIGN!

The shield on Axl's Tower Carrier (set 70322) is a scannable, rock-throwing NEXO Power.

Q | Do the NEXO KNIGHTS heroes ride horses?

A | Not just horses, but robot horses! Lance's Mecha Horse (set 70312) from 2016 is a huge robo-steed that can turn into a motorbike.

HEROES' HQ

The Fortrex (set 70317) is the NEXO KNIGHTS heroes' mobile base—a castle and a battle wagon all in one!

FIRST LEGO CASTLE ON WHEELS

The Fortrex (set 70317)

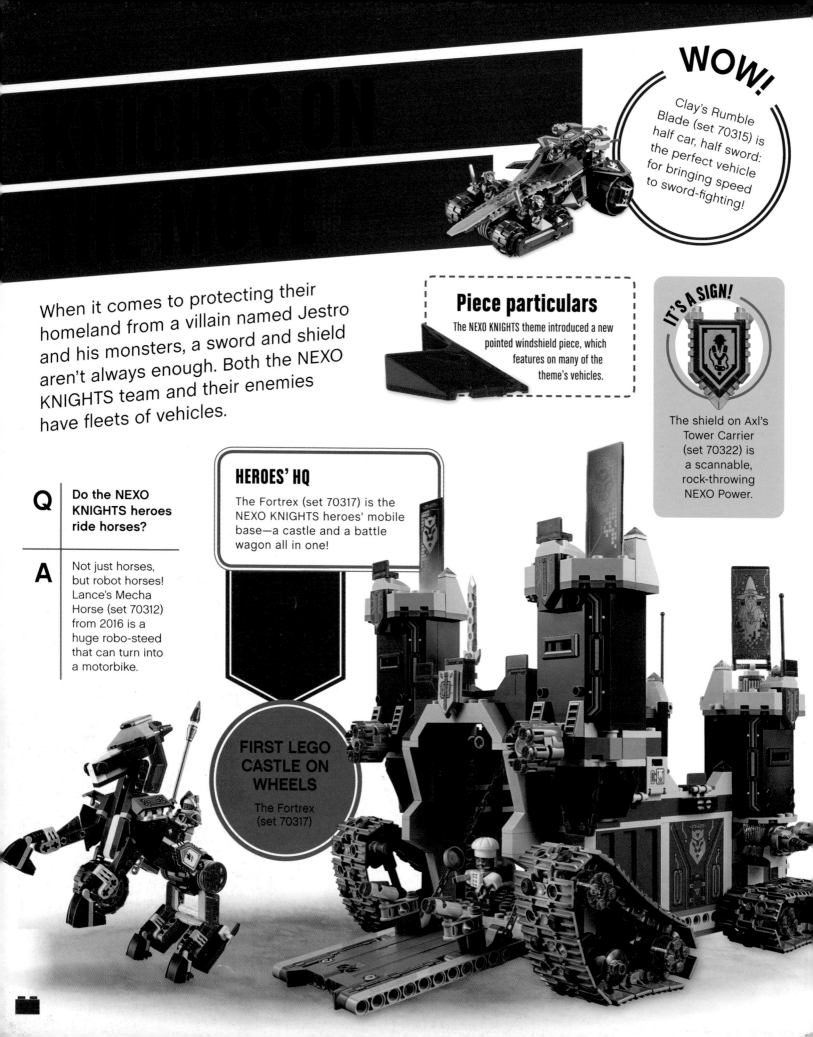

AWESOME!

You may have heard of horsepower, but what about lava power? Jestro's Evil Mobile (set 70316) is a two-wheeled ride pulled along by a hulking lava giant named Sparkks.

TOP 5
Mega mean machines

1 General Magmar's Siege Machine of Doom (set 70321) rumbles along on six wheels or rises up to become a seige tower.

2 Jestro's Headquarters (set 70352) features colossal rocky wheels and a detachable stone boat.

3 Jestro's Evil Mobile (set 70316) has jaws that open and close as the vehicle moves.

4 Beast Master's Chaos Chariot (set 70314) is pulled along by two giant, snapping Globlins.

5 Ruina's Lock & Roller (set 70349) has a jail cell that opens when you push the Forbidden Power shield.

EVIL ROAD TRIP, ANYONE?

LOOK CLOSER

Jestro based the design of the front part of his Evil Mobile (set 70316) on a freakish jester's hat.

TO THE MOON AND BACK

While the LEGO Space theme explored the realms of science-fiction, many other LEGO sets have explored real-world space exploration—even way back before the first real-life Moon landing in 1969!

FACT STACK

The first outer space LEGO set was a 115-piece rocket in 1964.

LEGO Town joined the space race in 1990, with the addition of its first space shuttle.

More than 40 LEGO sets have had a real-world space theme.

ER60079

KEY DATES

1973
Rocket Base (set 358) features a realistic rocket and command center, a year after NASA's last manned Moon mission.

1995
LEGO Town rivals NASA with its very own space program, in the subtheme Launch Command.

2003
The LEGO Group partners with Discovery Channel for six space sets, including a Lunar Lander (set 10029) with two Apollo astronauts.

2015
LEGO City gets a brand-new spaceport, plus a Training Jet Transporter (set 60079) for future shuttle pilots!

MARTIAN LEGO PIECES

To help compare colors picked up by their cameras in Martian daylight, NASA fitted red, blue, and yellow "LEGO plates" to its Mars rovers in 2003. The plates looked like real LEGO pieces, but they were made out of metal to survive in space.

LARGEST LEGO IDEAS SET

Apollo 11 Saturn V Rocket (set 21309) at 39in (1m) tall

LOOK CLOSER

The astronaut in 1999's Space Simulation Station (set 6455) is undergoing G-force training in this spinning set!

The LEGO NASA Mars Science Laboratory Curiosity Rover (set 21104) was designed by real-life NASA engineer Stephen Pakbaz.

LEGO Technic Space Shuttle (set 8480)

1,366 pieces
Including a 9-volt motor

6 fiber-optic cables
For lighting the engine exhausts

2 motorized bay doors
Built with angled beam pieces—new in 1996!

1 working crane arm
For launching the on-board satellite

AWESOME!

5,304,140

Miles (8,536,186km) traveled by a LEGO model of the space shuttle *Discovery* in 2010, while on board the real NASA space shuttle *Discovery*.

I HOPE I DON'T HAVE HELMET HAIR

Brick History

In 1975, Space Module with Astronauts (set 367) replicated a Moon landing with three brick-built spacemen, whose helmets could be swapped for faces.

Stardefender 200
(set 6932)

A HISTORY OF THE FUTURE

LEGO Space has changed a lot over the years, but one thing ties all the eras together and that's spaceships spaceships, SPACESHIPS

1980s

New-look white exploration vessels continue to research the universe, while Space Police are on patrol for notorious Blacktron craft.

1990s

Flying saucers and alien insects are just some of the strange sights to be spotted deeper into space.

Galactic Peace Keeper (set 6886)

Xenon X-Craft
(set 6872)

Space Transporter
(set 924)

Space Dart I
(set 6824)

Insectoid Son Stinger (set 6?

1970s

The first LEGO astronauts blast off in blue and gray ships that don't stray too far from scientific fact.

Space Scooter
(set 885)

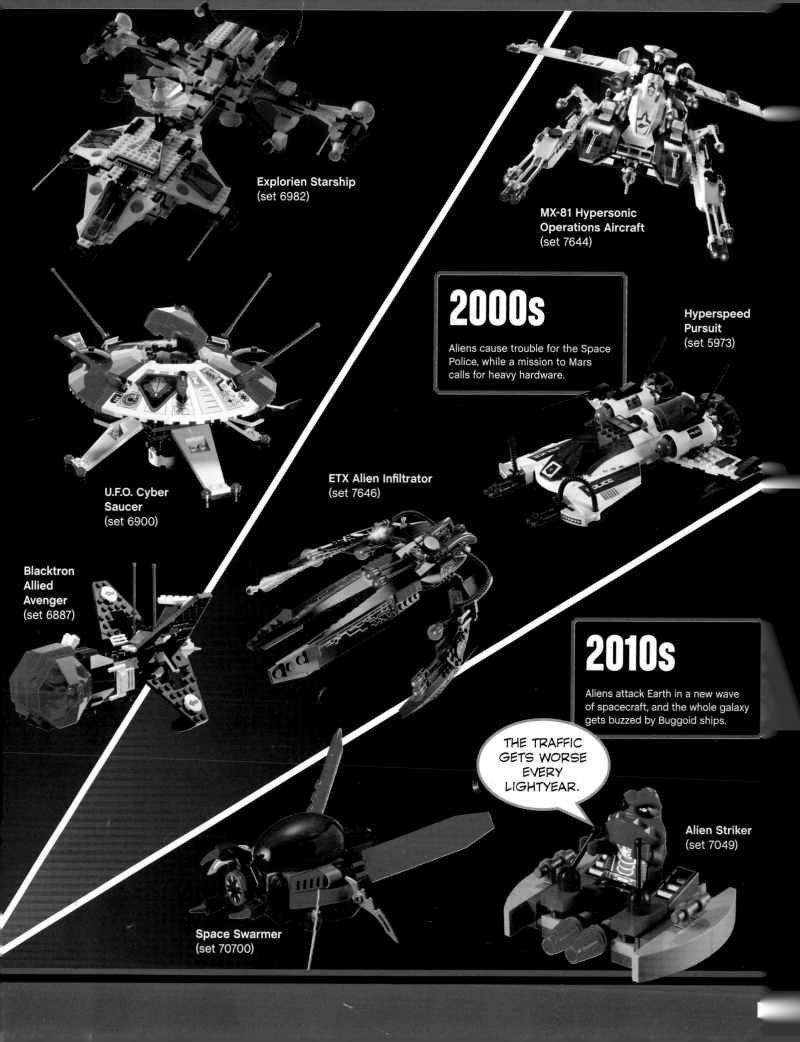

Explorien Starship
(set 6982)

MX-81 Hypersonic
Operations Aircraft
(set 7644)

2000s

Aliens cause trouble for the Space Police, while a mission to Mars calls for heavy hardware.

Hyperspeed Pursuit
(set 5973)

U.F.O. Cyber Saucer
(set 6900)

ETX Alien Infiltrator
(set 7646)

Blacktron Allied Avenger
(set 6887)

2010s

Aliens attack Earth in a new wave of spacecraft, and the whole galaxy gets buzzed by Buggoid ships.

THE TRAFFIC GETS WORSE EVERY LIGHTYEAR.

Alien Striker
(set 7049)

Space Swarmer
(set 70700)

PARKING SPACE

Spaceships aren't the only way to get around the galaxy! With the help of wheels and walkers, LEGO astronauts have charted strange new worlds in these tough land-based vehicles.

I'M THE TREADED GALACTIC TITAN!

I'M WHEELY AWESOME.

FACT STACK

Moon buggies featured in all four of the first LEGO Space sets in 1978.

More than 100 LEGO Space sets feature wheels.

Mono Jet (set 7310) is the only LEGO Space vehicle to run on only one wheel.

12

Wheels on the giant Roboforce Robomaster (set 2154) from 1997.

TOP 5
Robotic rides

1 Robot Command Center (set 6951)

2 Alien Moon Stalker (set 6940)

3 Spyrius Robo Guardian (set 6949)

4 Life on Mars Recon Mech (set 7314)

5 Galaxy Squad Star Slicer (set 70703)

AWESOME!

The centerpiece of the Space subtheme Futuron was the battery-powered Monorail Transport System (set 6990), which had more than 10ft (3m) of "Space Trak."

START THE SPACE ENGINES!

Brick statistics

Solar Power Transporter
(set 6952)

6 large wheels
Fit sideways under cockpits during flight

4 astronauts
And one friendly droid fit in the vehicle

2 cockpits
Detachable from the front and back

2 space engines
Attach to cockpits to make spaceships

1 control room
Stands freely on fold-down struts

LOST IN SPACE

This six-wheeled satellite-launcher was designed in the 1980s but never released. A single prototype box is kept securely in the LEGO Group archives.

GET ME TO A GALAXY FAR, FAR AWAY!

The LEGO® *Star Wars*™ theme has been flying high for nearly 20 years, and these are just some of the spaceships that have taken it to new heights.

386
Black pieces in Krennic's Imperial Shuttle (set 75156).

FACT STACK

The first LEGO *Star Wars* spaceships launched in 1999.

More than 150 LEGO *Star Wars* spaceships have been released to date.

Almost 100 sets are based on ships from the *Star Wars* movies.

More than 50 ships are inspired by *Star Wars* TV shows and games.

Piece particulars

Not all LEGO *Star Wars* flying machines are futuristic! Wicket the Ewok flies a glider made with fishing rod pieces in The Battle of Endor (set 8038).

Brick statistics

18 TIE fighters
Released at minifigure scale, including TIE variants

7 X-wing fighters
At minifigure scale, including Poe Dameron's X-wing

5 *Millennium Falcons*
At minifigure scale, including one Ultimate Collector's set

3 Imperial Shuttles
At minifigure scale, including one Ultimate Collector's set

GETTING FROM A TO Y

Lots of *Star Wars* ships are named for their resemblance to letters, and every single one has been spelled out in LEGO bricks.

B IS FOR...
B-Wing (set 75050)

A IS FOR...
A-Wing (set 75175)

U IS FOR...
U-Wing (set 75155)

1 *Slave I* (set 7144), 2000

2 Jango Fett's *Slave I* (set 7153), 2002

3 *Slave I* (set 6209), 2006

4 Mini *Slave I* (*Star Wars* Celebration V Exclusive), 2012

5 Ultimate Collector's Series *Slave I* (set 75060), 2015

AWESOME!

The LEGO *Star Wars Rebels* Wookiee Gunship (set 75084) from 2015 was the first Wookiee spaceship and the first set to feature rapid-fire stud shooters.

Imperial measures

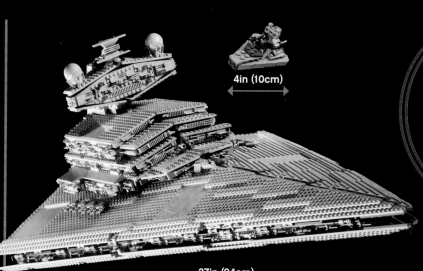

4in (10cm)

37in (94cm)

Imperial Star Destroyer Ultimate Collector's version
(set 10030)
3,104 pieces, 37in (94cm) long

Imperial Star Destroyer Microfighter version
(set 75033)
97 pieces, 4in (10cm) long

WOW!

Count Dooku's Solar Sailer (set 7752) from LEGO *Star Wars: The Clone Wars* has sails that spread out like flower petals to soak up solar rays.

REALLY?!

Luke Skywalker's X-Wing Fighter (set 4502) from 2004 comes covered in Dagobah swamp gunk.

X IS FOR...
X-Wing (set 75149)

Y IS FOR...
Y-Wing (set 9495)

V IS FOR...
V-Wing (set 75039)

GROUND WARS

The LEGO *Star Wars* saga stretches across more than just space. In worlds of sand, snow, forest, and fire, ingenious ground vehicles are required to get around.

REALLY?!

TIE fighters aren't only found in the sky! The TIE Crawler (set 7664) from 2007 runs on caterpillar tracks.

WAY TO GO!

There are almost as many ways to get around a planet as there are planets to get around! All you need to do is pick a mode of propulsion...

Q | I need a speeder bike for my trip to Endor but I don't like brown. Can you help me?

A | Certainly! As well as brown, speeder bikes are also available in red, white, and green.

TRACK POWER

Half tank, half droid, the Corporate Alliance Tank Droid (set 75015) crawls along on a single caterpillar track.

LEG POWER

Captain Rex's AT-TE (set 75157) from LEGO *Star Wars Rebels* has been modified from a walking weapon to a home.

Brick History

In 2007, a Motorized Walking AT-AT (set 10178) strode onto the scene. It could be set to walk forward or backward at the flick of a switch.

BABY STEPS

Since 2014, LEGO *Star Wars* Microfighters have depicted classic *Star Wars* craft such as the AT-DP (set 75130), using just a handful of pieces each.

WOW!

Republic Dropship with AT-OT Walker (set 10195) is an airship and walker all in one. It is the biggest LEGO *Star Wars: The Clone Wars* set, with 1,758 pieces.

15

Pieces used to make Luke's landspeeder in the 2014 LEGO *Star Wars* Advent Calendar.

BEST UNICYCLIST

General Grievous on his Wheel Bike (set 75040)

WHEEL POWER

The 10-wheeled Clone Turbo Tank (set 8098) has more wheels than any other LEGO *Star Wars* vehicle, plus working suspension.

I APPEAR TO BE GOING THE WRONG WAY.

POD POWER

Anakin Skywalker's homemade Podracer (set 7962) is nearly all engine, with just a small seat for a pilot pulled along behind.

ULTRA COOL SETS

Unbelievably Complex Spaceships? Utterly Convincing Sculptures? In the LEGO *Star Wars* theme, UCS stands for Ultimate Collector's Series. These are some of the most advanced LEGO sets in the galaxy!

TIE Interceptor
(set 7181)

Start here!

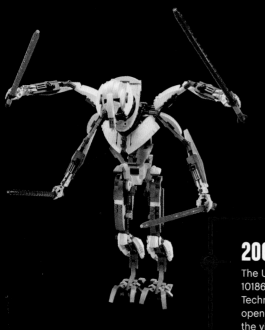

2008

The UCS **General Grievous** (set 10186) is made primarily from LEGO Technic pieces. It features an opening chest plate that reveals the villain's cyborg innards.

2007

The Ultimate Collector's Series *Millennium Falcon* (set 10179) is the first UCS set to come with minifigures, as the range begins to include more play features.

The Ultimate Collector's Series **R2-D2** (set 10225) has 2,127 pieces and is more than 200 times bigger than a minifigure-scale Artoo!

2012

2010

Imperial Shuttle (set 10212), not only includes five minifigures, it is also the first UCS set to be built at the same scale as its pilots and passengers.

X-Wing Fighter
(set 7191)

Looming 17in (43cm) tall,
the UCS **Darth Maul Bust**
(set 10018) is almost as
large as life—and just as scary.

2001

2000

The Ultimate Collector's Series launches with
a 703-piece **TIE Interceptor** (set 7181) and a
1,304-piece **X-Wing Fighter** (set 7191).

2002

The first-ever set to have more
than 3,000 pieces, the huge
UCS **Imperial Star Destroyer**
(set 10030) also comes with
a tiny Rebel blockade runner.

2005

The UCS **Death Star II** from
Return of the Jedi (set 10143)
is both the first LEGO
Death Star and the largest,
with a circumference
of 60in (152cm).

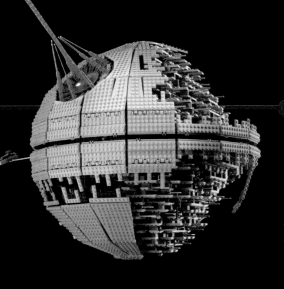

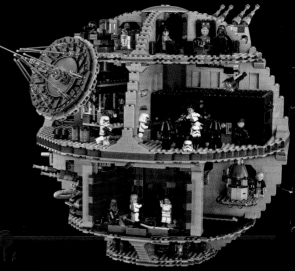

2014

With more play features
than ever, the **UCS
Sandcrawler** (set 75059)
features working cranes
and steering, eight
opening sections,
seven minifigures,
and six droids.

2016

The latest version of the **Death Star**
(set 75159) features details that take
the piece count to more than 4,000.

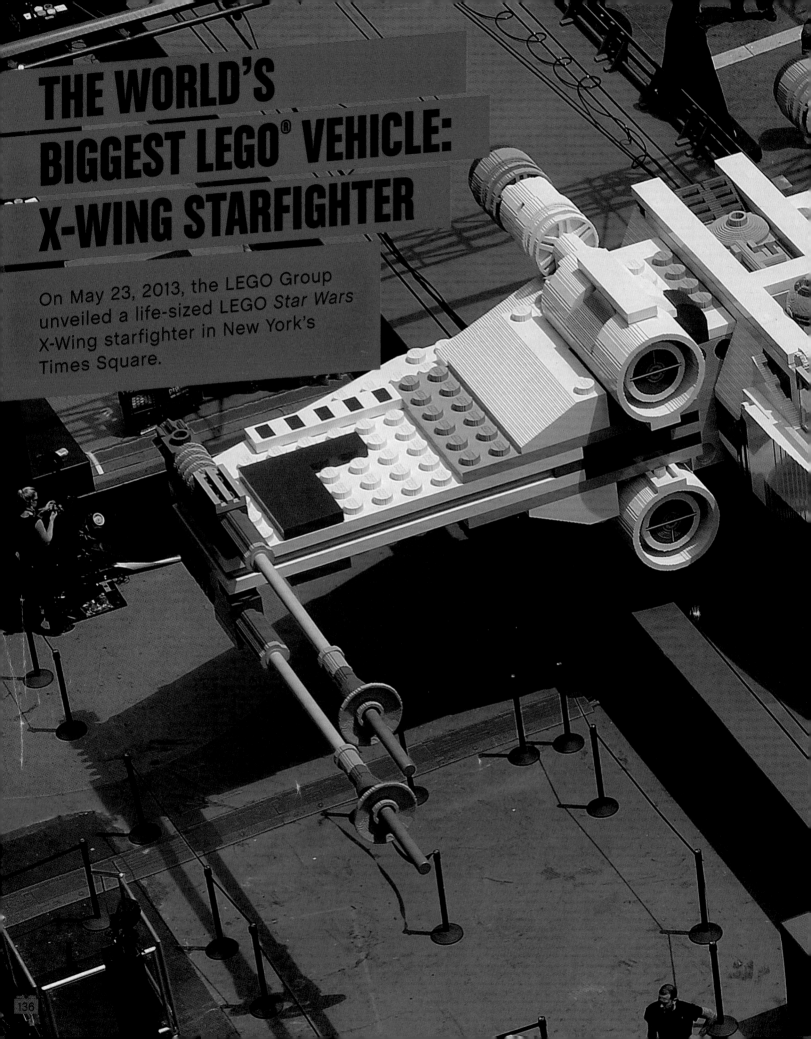

THE WORLD'S BIGGEST LEGO® VEHICLE: X-WING STARFIGHTER

On May 23, 2013, the LEGO Group unveiled a life-sized LEGO Star Wars X-Wing starfighter in New York's Times Square.

Brick statistics

5,335,200 bricks
Weighing 45,980lbs (20,865kg)

32 LEGO master builders
Worked on it in the LEGO Model Shop
in Kladno, Czech Republic

43ft (13.1m) long
With a 44ft (13.4m) wingspan

42 times bigger
Than the X-Wing Starfighter set (set 9493)
on which it is based

17,336 hours to build
That's about four months!

FANTASTIC VOYAGERS

There's more to LEGO vehicles than City cars and spaceships—just ask the drivers of these fantasy dream machines!

AND YOU THOUGHT I WAS EXTINCT!

Q Why does Maula's Ice Mammoth Stomper (set 70145) have propellers on its sides?

A Because this LEGO Legends of Chima set is actually two vehicles in one: a huge, woolly mammoth-like walker and a smaller, folding flyer that wraps across its back!

LEGO EXO-FORCE Mobile Devastator (set 8108)

1,009 parts
Including four giant, bright green wheels

23.5in (60cm) long
And 13.5in (34cm) tall

10 robot warriors on board
Including robot leader Meca One

2 detachable robot scout ships
Connected to the elevating battle tower

1 hero stands in its way
In his Blazing Falcon battle machine!

NO MEDALS! CAN'T YOU SEE I'M UNDERCOVER?

MOST INAPPROPRIATELY NAMED VEHICLE

LEGO Ultra Agents Stealth Patrol (set 70169)

AWESOME!

In a world of hay carts and horses, Troll Battle Wheel (set 7041) is the most way-out weapon LEGO Castle has ever seen!

WOW!

When battling the LEGO® Alpha Team, evil Ogel's Scorpion Orb Launcher (set 4774) can stand up on its mighty stinger to attack!

LOOK CLOSER

The printed face on the front of the LEGO® Monster Fighters Ghost Train (set 9467) looks even scarier when you see it glowing in the dark!

BRICK CHALLENGE

Think of the wackiest way to get around, then build it with your LEGO bricks!

6

Legs on the creepy-crawly LEGO® BIONICLE Toa Terrain Crawler (set 8927).

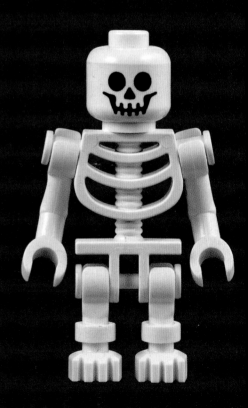

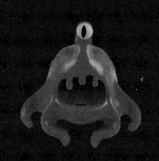

CHAPTER FOUR

MINIFIGURES, MONSTERS, AND MORE

SMALL BEGINNINGS

In 1978, the first minifigures added new character to the worlds of LEGO sets. Their insistent smiles and ingenious design made them an instant hit.

FACT STACK

Out of the LEGO colors available in 1978, yellow was chosen for minifigures as it was considered the best choice to represent all skin tones.

The fundamental minifigure form has not changed since it was perfected in 1978.

The unique design of the LEGO minifigure was first protected by a patent in Denmark in 1977.

Since 2000, the distinctive minifigure shape has been recognized as a trademark.

I LIKE YOUR HAIR.

I LIKE *YOUR* HAIR!

REALLY?!

Until 1983, there were only two minifigure haircuts: pigtails and side parting. There have been more than 200 styles since.

TORSO COUTURE

The first minifigures had plain torsos that could be decorated with stickers. Printed torsos were introduced later in 1978, starting with a Train Conductor.

40

Minifigure variants were released in 1978. Today there are more than 8,000!

TOP 5

Early minifigure tools still in use today

1 Axe
(1978)

2 Sword
(1978)

3 Shovel
(1978)

4 Radio
(1979)

5 Wrench
(1979)

Q What are LEGO minifigures made from?

A Just like LEGO bricks, minifigures are made from a tough plastic compound called acrylonitrile butadiene styrene, known as ABS for short.

WOW!

A team of LEGO designers, led by Jens Nygård Knudsen, made 50 different minifigure prototypes from plastic and tin before arriving at the final design.

LOOK CLOSER

675

SNACK BAR

LEGO

snack bar

The boxes of several 1979 sets show minifigures wearing a hair piece that was never released. The final element was more intricately shaped to suggest ears.

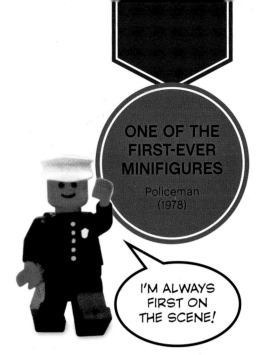

ONE OF THE FIRST-EVER MINIFIGURES

Policeman (1978)

I'M ALWAYS FIRST ON THE SCENE!

MAYBE BABIES

As well as appearing as adults in LEGOLAND® sets, some of the first minifigures were cast as infants in larger scale LEGO Homemaker sets, alongside tall "building figures."

THE MAKING OF A MINIFIGURE

THE DESIGN PROCESS

It can take a whole year to design and make a minifigure! From coming up with new ideas to testing the finished product, every step is vital to make each minifigure the best it can be…

1 MAKING A START

The LEGO Group has a dedicated design team for minifigures. Its members work closely with set designers to help each model tell its story with the right collection of characters.

2 FIGURING IT OUT

The design team starts by brainstorming ideas, making rough sketches by hand, and doing research—for example, visiting a firehouse if they are designing firefighters.

WHAT ABOUT MY PANTS?

3 PICTURING THE PIECES

Next, graphic designers work on a blank minifigure template to refine and develop the initial sketches, choosing colors for different body parts, and adding more detail to facial features and clothing.

4 MINIFIGURE MODELING

If a design calls for a new hair piece, accessory, or body part, an element designer sculpts an extra-large version out of clay, or makes a virtual 3-D computer model. This allows the sculptor to create the finer details for each piece.

MINIFIGURE, OR NOT?

Many LEGO themes feature minifigure characters, but not every character in those themes is a minifigure! Characters made from non-standard parts are known as "creature figures" and come in lots of different shapes and sizes.

This **policeman** is a minifigure because he has all the standard minifigure parts: torso, arms, legs, and a head.

This **skeleton** is classed as a creature figure, not a minifigure, because it does not have a standard torso or any standard limbs.

This **Scurrier** is also classed as a creature figure because it does not have any standard minifigure parts at all!

The classic minifigure form has not changed since 1978, but the details and decorations that make each one special still offer plenty of scope for new ideas.

NOW I'M READY FOR BATTLE!

9

SAFETY ASSURED
A new minifigure goes through many different safety checks before it is approved for production, including stress tests and risk assessments.

7

SECRET STANDARDS
Every step of the way, the team must make sure their creation conforms to secret LEGO minifigure design guidelines that ensure quality and consistency across the whole LEGO range.

EXPERT OPINIONS
Throughout the process, pictures and prototypes of the new minifigure may be shown to children to get their opinions on its design and playability.

8

INTO PRODUCTION
When approved by the design team, product safety team, and others, the minifigure can finally be sent to the factory for production.

10

6

THE BIG PICTURE
Next, a small number of prototype pieces are made at actual size. Stickers showing the graphics are added, and all elements of the design are reviewed as a complete package.

5

UPLOADING...
When a clay sculpt (known as a maquette) is finished, it is scanned into a computer and adjusted to make sure its dimensions fit perfectly with existing LEGO elements.

MAKING FACES
Though modern minifigures have many different faces, their features all conform to strict design rules. This means they can be easily identified and all of them can wear the same hats, helmets, masks, and hair pieces.

Most minifigures have black eyes, but some non-human characters have colored eyes.

Most minifigure children are designed with bigger than average eyes and freckles to distinguish them from adults.

Minifigures with scared or unhappy faces usually have a happy face printed on the other side of their head.

9,610,000,000

Approximate distance from the Earth to the Moon, measured in minifigures.

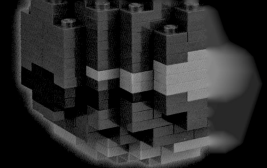

Brick History

In 2008, all five colors of the classic space minifigure were reissued to celebrate 30 years of minifigures. All wore modern helmets, but without visors.

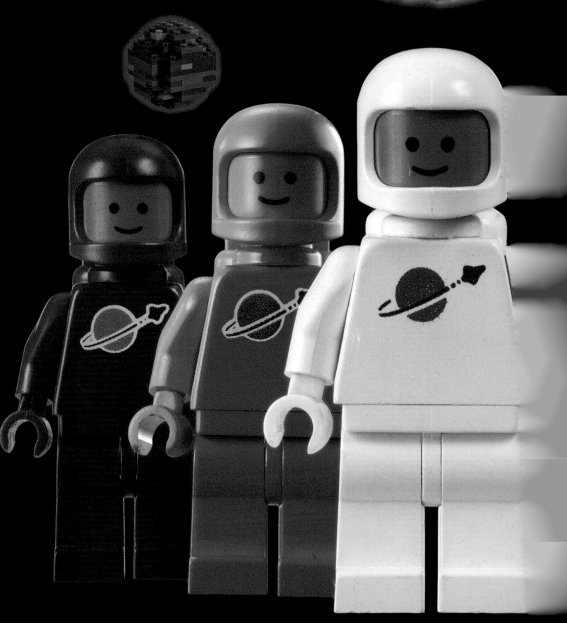

FACT STACK

In 1978, the first LEGO space minifigures wore either red or white outfits.

Yellow spacesuits appeared in 1979 then blue and black in 1984.

Black spacesuits are the rarest, appearing in fewer than 10 sets.

The most recent sets feature astronauts in red, blue, green, and orange.

KEY DATES

1987
The LEGO® Futuron space minifigures are the first to get helmets with transparent visors.

1992
The first LEGO Space minifigures to have special face prints appear in Space Police sets.

1993
Ice Planet 2002 sets are the first to distinguish between male and female astronauts.

2011
Space minifigures get double-sided face prints so they can look alarmed in Alien Conquest sets!

AWESOME!

Classic-style space minifigures didn't wear green until 2014's Exo Suit (set 21109), a fan-designed LEGO® Ideas set.

In 2003, pictures of two "Astrobot" minifigures, Biff and Sandy, were sent to Mars on real spaceships.

BROKEN BENNY

Benny from the THE LEGO® MOVIE™ was based on the original blue Space minifigure from 1984. His helmet was designed to look like it was broken due to it being played with a great deal, for that authentic toybox vibe!

IT'S A SIGN!

The classic LEGO Space logo is still in use after almost 40 years.

BRICK CHALLENGE

Try building a LEGO planet for your astronaut minifigures to explore, like this inspirational model.

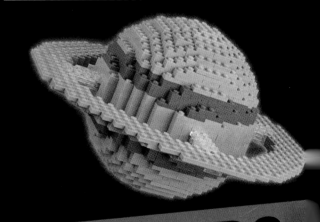

FLYING COLORS

Red alert! And yellow! And blue! In 1978, these explorers made a giant leap for LEGO minifigures. Boldly going where no bricks had gone before, they were the first to venture into LEGOLAND Space. They have remained beloved figures for lightyears since.

MINIFIGURES THROUGH THE AGES

LEGO® Minifigures have taken inspiration from historical (and prehistorical) humans from as early as 10,000 BCE. These characters range from cavemen to modern starlets and scientists.

Start here!

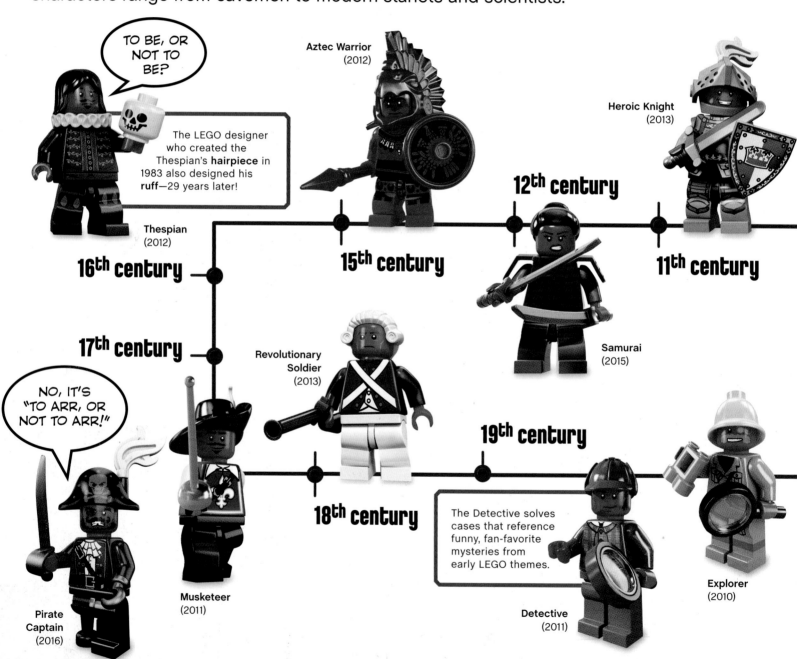

TO BE, OR NOT TO BE?

The LEGO designer who created the Thespian's **hairpiece** in 1983 also designed his **ruff**—29 years later!

Thespian
(2012)

Aztec Warrior
(2012)

Heroic Knight
(2013)

12ᵗʰ century

16ᵗʰ century

15ᵗʰ century

11ᵗʰ century

17ᵗʰ century

Samurai
(2015)

Revolutionary Soldier
(2013)

NO, IT'S "TO ARR, OR NOT TO ARR!"

19ᵗʰ century

18ᵗʰ century

The Detective solves cases that reference funny, fan-favorite mysteries from early LEGO themes.

Musketeer
(2011)

Pirate Captain
(2016)

Detective
(2011)

Explorer
(2010)

WE COME IN PIECES!

In the LEGO Space universe, aliens and robots come in many shapes and sizes. Some are peaceful, but others are preparing for battle!

IT'S A SIGN!

The cyborg Space Villain from the LEGO Minifigures line wears a green "B" symbol, first used by Blacktron crooks in 1991's LEGO Space sets.

MEET THE MARTIANS

In 2001, LEGO® Life on Mars sets mixed astronauts with brand-new Martian figures. These friendly aliens featured new parts and colors and were named after real stars and constellations.

MY NAME IS VEGA.

Q | Who was the first alien minifigure?

A | Alpha Draconis and his fellow U.F.O. aliens made first contact in 1996. They wore unique, out-of-this-world helmets, with scary printed faces underneath.

Top 5

Cosmic citizen collectibles

1. **Space Alien** (Series 3, 2011)

2. **Classic Alien** (Series 6, 2012)

3. **Alien Trooper** (Series 13, 2015)

4. **Alien Villainess** (Series 8, 2011)

5. **Alien Avenger** (Series 9, 2013)

Space Alien   **Classic Alien**

REALLY?!

The spooky Space Skulls starred in a 2008 LEGO® Factory set, piloting giant, skull-shaped spaceships!

SMALLEST ALIEN

One-eyed Clinger from Alien Conquest sets

Brick History

The first minifigure designed to represent a robot was the Spyrius Droid from 1994. He was also the first minifigure to have printed legs.

245633

The prisoner number of escaped alien crook Jawson, who was on the loose in LEGO Space Police sets during 2010.

Alien Trooper

Alien Villainess

Alien Avenger

THE MAGIC OF MINIFIGURES

Every minifigure has a touch of magic, but these wizards, enchanters, witches, and wish-granters have a little bit more than most.

Brick History

In 2012, the LEGO® *The Lord of the Rings*™ and *The Hobbit*™ themes launched, reimagining magical characters such as Gandalf the Grey in minifigure form.

REALLY?!

In the LEGO® NINJAGO® world, magical, wish-granting beings known as djinn inhabit a parallel realm called... Djinjago!

MYTHS AND LEG-ENDS

The magical, mystical Faun from the LEGO Minifigures theme has a special leg piece used in no other set. Though his goat-like limbs are slim, his hooves still fit onto LEGO studs.

Q Can you still get LEGO *Harry Potter* sets?

A Though the LEGO® *Harry Potter*™ theme came to an end in 2011, minifigure versions of Harry, Hermione, and Lord Voldemort are still having magical adventures in the LEGO® DIMENSIONS™ theme.

BRICK CHALLENGE

Build a LEGO box with a hidden compartment to make a disappearing minifigure magic trick!

PICK A POTTER

There are many different minifigure versions of Harry Potter, yet each one shares the same familiar lightning-bolt scar!

GOATEE BEARD? I'VE GOT A GOATY *EVERYTHING!*

TOP 5

LEGO Minifigures conjurors

1 Fairy
(Series 8, 2012)

2 Leprechaun
(Series 6, 2012)

3 Wizard
(Series 12, 2014)

4 Genie Girl
(Series 12, 2014)

5 Wacky Witch
(Series 14, 2015)

8

Different wizards have appeared in LEGO Castle sets since 1995.

WOW!

Amset-Ra is the Pharaoh at the heart of 2011's Pharaoh's Quest theme. His six magical treasures are guarded by enchanted warriors such as Flying Mummies.

MINIFIGURE FIRSTS

These pioneers have all earned their place in history by taking LEGO minifigures into new areas of innovation, fashion, and play!

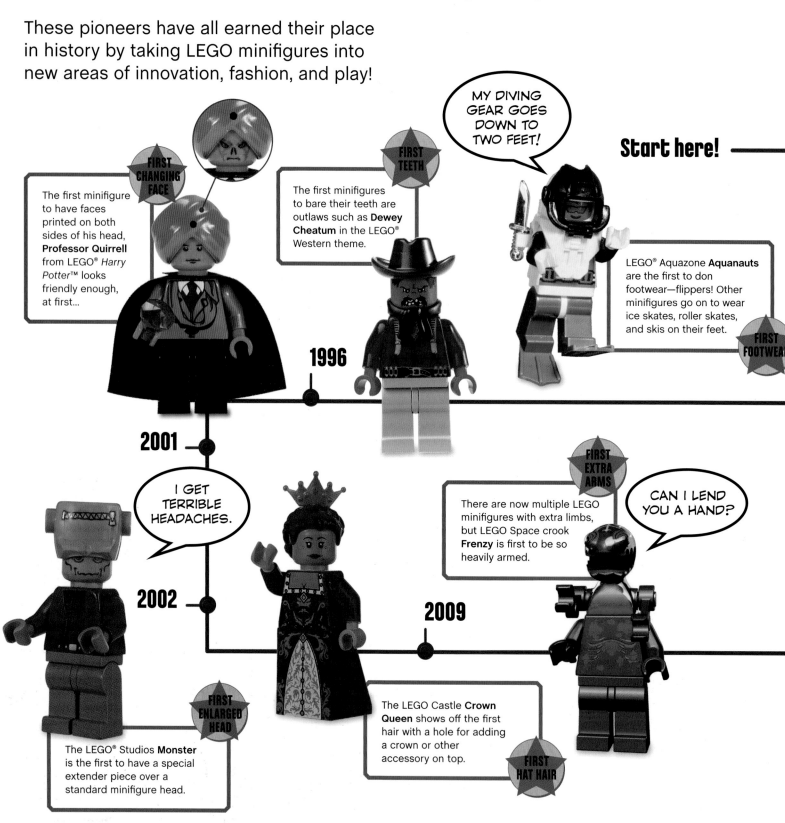

FIRST CHANGING FACE

The first minifigure to have faces printed on both sides of his head, **Professor Quirrell** from LEGO® *Harry Potter*™ looks friendly enough, at first...

FIRST TEETH

The first minifigures to bare their teeth are outlaws such as **Dewey Cheatum** in the LEGO® Western theme.

MY DIVING GEAR GOES DOWN TO TWO FEET!

Start here!

LEGO® Aquazone **Aquanauts** are the first to don footwear—flippers! Other minifigures go on to wear ice skates, roller skates, and skis on their feet.

FIRST FOOTWEAR

1996

2001

I GET TERRIBLE HEADACHES.

2002

FIRST EXTRA ARMS

There are now multiple LEGO minifigures with extra limbs, but LEGO Space crook **Frenzy** is first to be so heavily armed.

CAN I LEND YOU A HAND?

2009

FIRST ENLARGED HEAD

The LEGO® Studios **Monster** is the first to have a special extender piece over a standard minifigure head.

The LEGO Castle **Crown Queen** shows off the first hair with a hole for adding a crown or other accessory on top.

FIRST HAT HAIR

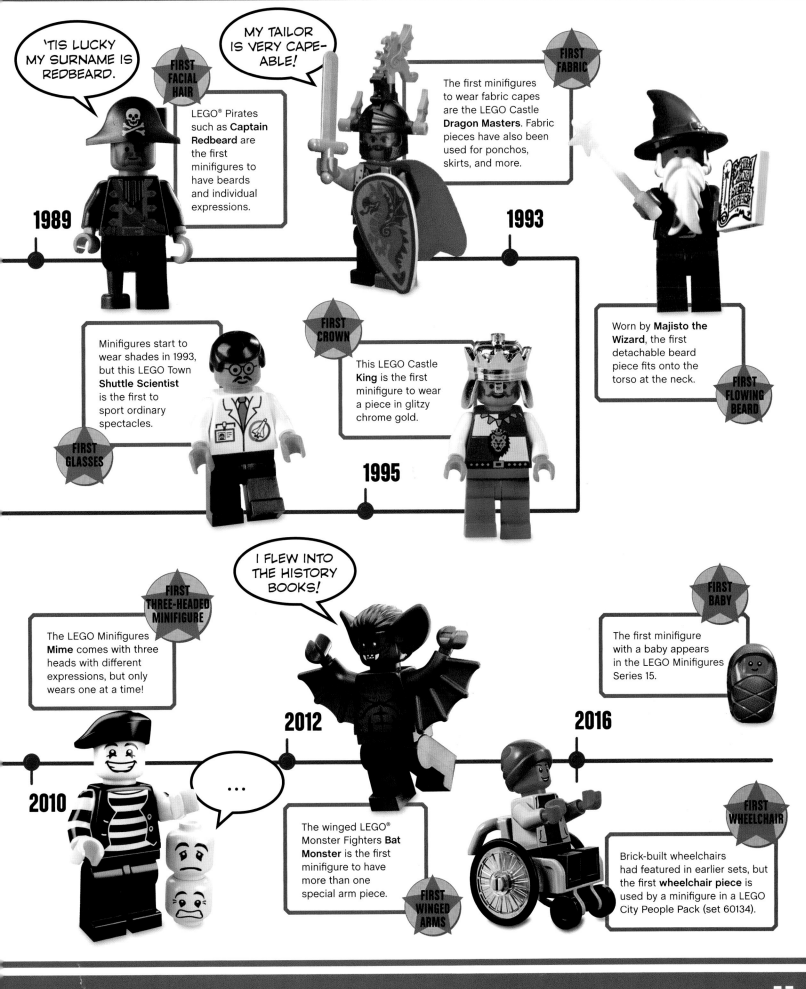

'TIS LUCKY MY SURNAME IS REDBEARD.

MY TAILOR IS VERY CAPE-ABLE!

FIRST FACIAL HAIR

LEGO® Pirates such as **Captain Redbeard** are the first minifigures to have beards and individual expressions.

FIRST FABRIC

The first minifigures to wear fabric capes are the LEGO Castle **Dragon Masters**. Fabric pieces have also been used for ponchos, skirts, and more.

1989

1993

Minifigures start to wear shades in 1993, but this LEGO Town **Shuttle Scientist** is the first to sport ordinary spectacles.

FIRST GLASSES

FIRST CROWN

This LEGO Castle **King** is the first minifigure to wear a piece in glitzy chrome gold.

Worn by **Majisto the Wizard**, the first detachable beard piece fits onto the torso at the neck.

FIRST FLOWING BEARD

1995

FIRST THREE-HEADED MINIFIGURE

The LEGO Minifigures **Mime** comes with three heads with different expressions, but only wears one at a time!

I FLEW INTO THE HISTORY BOOKS!

FIRST BABY

The first minifigure with a baby appears in the LEGO Minifigures Series 15.

2012

2016

2010

...

The winged LEGO® Monster Fighters **Bat Monster** is the first minifigure to have more than one special arm piece.

FIRST WINGED ARMS

FIRST WHEELCHAIR

Brick-built wheelchairs had featured in earlier sets, but the first **wheelchair piece** is used by a minifigure in a LEGO City People Pack (set 60134).

THE WILD BUNCH

These LEGO characters are no ordinary creatures. In their play themes, animals talk, wear clothes, and have amazing adventures!

Eagles
Other tribes of birds include the Ravens and the Vultures.

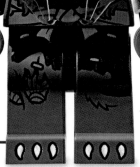

FACT STACK

The first LEGO® DUPLO® animal figures were a dog and a cat, found in several 1970s sets.

Unikitty from THE LEGO® MOVIE™ is a rare example of a brick-built animal character.

Licensed themes with animal characters include Mickey Mouse and Winnie the Pooh.

Two wolf-headed Anubis Warriors appear in 2011's Pharaoh's Quest theme.

27

Pieces used to build Spinlyn the Spider from LEGO® Legends of Chima™, making her the biggest minifigure ever!

FANTASTIC BEASTS

For centuries, explorers have searched for mythical animals. If they just checked out the LEGO Minifigures line, they would find a Minotaur, a Yeti, and the unmistakable tracks of a "Square Foot!"

Saber-toothed Tigers
One of two tribe species extinct in the real world, along with Mammoths.

Phoenixes
The only Legends of Chima tribe to be based on a mythical creature.

THIS SUIT CAME WITH A LARGE BILL!

TOP 5
Collectible critter costumes

1 Lizard Man (Series 5, 2011)

2 Bunny Suit Guy (Series 7, 2012)

3 Bumblebee Girl (Series 10, 2013)

4 Shark Suit Guy (Series 15, 2016)

5 Penguin Suit Guy (Series 16, 2016)

THE TRIBES OF CHIMA

Animals from 21 tribes appeared in LEGO Chima sets between 2013 and 2015, including…

Lions
One of 14 mammal tribes, alongside Wolves, Beavers, Bears, and Bats.

Crocodiles
The only other cold-blooded tribes are the Scorpions and Spiders.

Brick History

In 2016, six LEGO sets based on *The Angry Birds Movie* were packed full of plummeting piggy figures, plus brand new bird pieces to send barreling toward them.

AWESOME!

In 2013 and 2014, LEGO® Teenage Mutant Ninja Turtles sets featured minifigure turtles, plus rat, dog, fish, and alligator figures.

LOOK CLOSER

Most LEGO Legends of Chima animal heads fit over a standard minifigure head with two printed faces. This allows different expressions to show through the eyeholes.

Piece particulars

In 2011, new head and tail parts were created for Serpentine characters in the LEGO® NINJAGO® theme. The snaking tails have since been used in the LEGO® NEXO KNIGHTS™ range and LEGO Minifigures series.

FAB FRIENDS

The animal characters of LEGO® FABULAND® were the first LEGO figures to have individual names and stories. Between 1979 and 1989, more than 40 characters appeared in almost 100 sets, including…

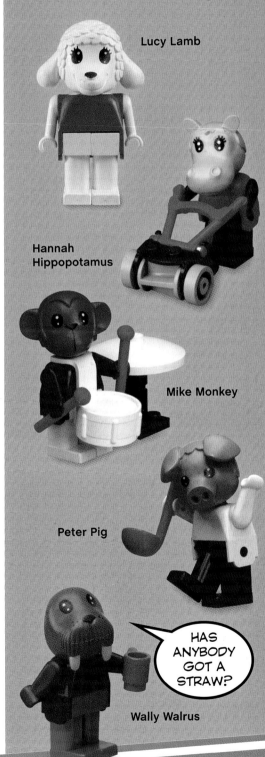

Lucy Lamb

Hannah Hippopotamus

Mike Monkey

Peter Pig

HAS ANYBODY GOT A STRAW?

Wally Walrus

Sea creatures

1 **LEGO shark** *(Squalus legodtus).*
Gray sharks were widespread in the
era of LEGO Pirates and can still be
seen in LEGO City harbor. White sharks
have also been spotted off LEGO Town.

2 **LEGO fish** *(Piscis legodtus).* The most common
variety of LEGO fish is silver-scaled, and ranges
as far as the LEGO® *Star Wars*™ universe.
Look out for orange and green species, too.

3 **LEGO octopus** *(Octopus legodtus).*
Black and red varieties of LEGO octopus
have been spotted by LEGO Pirates and
others, but only the LEGO® Agents have
identified a glow-in-the-dark one!

4 **LEGO crab** *(Carcinus legodtus).* Red crabs
are local to LEGO® BELVILLE™, but light
orange examples range across LEGO City,
Heartlake City, Ninjago Island, and elsewhere.

5 **LEGO crocodile** *(Crocodylus legodtus).*
First discovered by LEGO Pirates,
crocodiles have also been spotted by
LEGO® Adventurers in the jungle, and
explorers in the LEGO Town Outback.

Mammals

6 **LEGO horse** *(Equus legodtus).* The
horse is one of the most widespread
LEGO species. Since 2012, a more
athletic breed—given to rearing—
has become the dominant variety.

7 **LEGO cat** *(Felis legodta).* LEGO cats
are most popular as pets in LEGO
BELVILLE, but can also be seen alongside
LEGO witches and being rescued
from trees by LEGO City firefighters.

8 **LEGO dog** *(Canis legodtus).* Huskies,
Chihuahuas, Dalmatians, and terriers
are just some of the LEGO dog breeds
to be seen in LEGO City or further
afield with LEGO minifigure owners.

LEGO®

ANIMALS

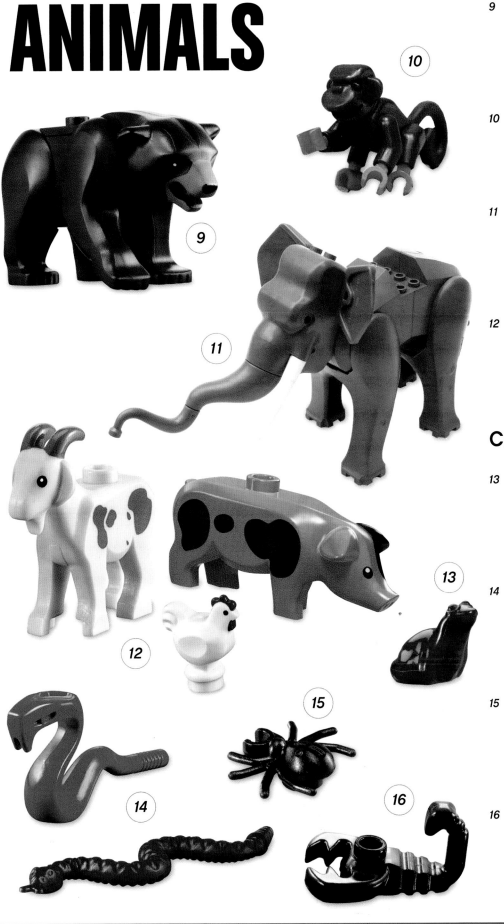

9   **LEGO bear** *(Ursus legodtus).* LEGO Town Arctic explorers were the first to encounter polar bears, while the LEGO City Forest Police have regular run-ins with mighty brown bears.

10   **LEGO monkey** *(Simius legodtus).* Abundant in the era of LEGO Pirates, a small number of LEGO monkeys also go about their business in LEGO Town and LEGO BELVILLE.

11   **LEGO elephant** *(Elefantus legodtus).* Only the LEGO Adventurers have encountered LEGO elephants. Though very rare, they are also very large, so if there is one to be seen, you won't miss it!

12   **LEGO farm animals** *(Domesticus legodtus).* LEGO goats, pigs, chickens, and cows were all reared in the LEGO Castle era, with pigs and cows still a familiar sight in certain areas of LEGO City.

Creepy crawlies

13   **LEGO frog** *(Rana legodta).* Frogs abound in a variety of LEGO environments, from the era of LEGO Castle to modern Heartlake City. They have even made the giant leap into LEGO Space!

14   **LEGO snake** *(Serpens legodtus).* The common LEGO snake spans many habitats and is most often colored red. Its fanged cousin comes in many colors and is largely restricted to Ninjago Island.

15   **LEGO spider** *(Aranea legodta).* More than 10 different colors of spider have been seen across a range of LEGO habitats, including glow-in-the-dark specimens found by LEGO Monster Fighters.

16   **LEGO scorpion** *(Scorpio legodtus).* Most often encountered by LEGO Adventurers, scorpions are also found on Ninjago Island. Rare, brightly colored varieties have been recorded further afield.

FASHION STATEMENTS

LEGO characters always dress to impress in a range of outfits, from the stylish to the outlandish. Here are some of their best and boldest fashion choices.

MOST LAID-BACK MINIFIGURE

The Dad from Ferris Wheel (set 10247)

2,642

The number of sets that black pants have been found in since they first appeared in 1978, making them the most popular pants for minifigures.

MY CAPE IS A LITTLE STIFF.

Piece particulars

The first LEGO capes were plastic pieces which mostly appeared on knight, king, and maiden minifigures from 1984 until 2003.

LOOK CLOSER

Some minifigures wear clothes that hark back to earlier LEGO eras. This funky top showing a classic LEGO astronaut appears in 14 sets.

AWESOME!

"Where Are My Pants?" Guy from THE LEGO MOVIE Minifigures range is more famous for the clothes he doesn't wear than the ones he does!

TOP 5
LEGO Minifigures in traditional costumes

1 Bagpiper (Series 7, 2012)

2 Flamenco Dancer (Series 6, 2012)

3 Hula Dancer (Series 3, 2011)

4 Lederhosen Guy (Series 8, 2012)

WOW!

There are three LEGO Minifigures who like to dress up as food: Hot Dog Man, Corn Cob Guy, and Banana Guy (pictured).

BUT YOU TOLD ME TO DRESS LIKE THIS...

MOST FASHIONABLE MINIFIGURE

Trendsetter

NO, I SAID WEAR SOMETHING APPEALING.

KEY DATES

1975
An early style in minifigure millinery, the **stetson**, or cowboy hat, can still be found in present-day sets.

1980
A chef is one of the first minifigures to wear a **top hat**! Most LEGO cooks since 1980 have opted for the more traditional chef's hat.

1989
Shiver me timbers! **Pirate hats** with and without skull and crossbones appear.

2001
Professor Quirrell from LEGO *Harry Potter* sets is the first to wear a **turban**.

2010
The Mime Artist wears the first LEGO **beret**, which has only ever appeared in black.

5 Kimono Girl
(Series 4, 2011)

Brick History

The very first male minifigures released in 1978 only wore hats until male LEGO hair pieces were invented in 1979.

A GALAXY OF STARS

From Han and Luke to Finn and Rey, the heroes of the *Star Wars* saga are some of the world's most iconic characters. They are all instantly recognizable as LEGO minifigures, too.

MOST UNDERDRESSED MINIFIGURE

Luke Skywalker (Bacta Tank variant, set 7879)

FACT STACK

In 2002, Yoda was the first LEGO minifigure to have short legs.

All new parts were needed to create the R2-D2 figure in 1999.

Jar Jar Binks was the first minifigure to have a specially shaped head mold.

There are 35 different minifigure versions of Luke Skywalker.

ROYAL EXCLUSIVE

Padmé Amidala wears her full Queen of Naboo regalia in Gungan Sub (set 9499). Her circular skirt has never been used in any other set.

I'VE GOT A GOOD FEELING ABOUT YOU, KID!

50

Approximate age difference in years between Young and Old Han Solo.

IT'S A SIGN!

Graffiti artist Sabine Wren from *Star Wars Rebels* wears a starbird icon of her own design. A similar emblem later becomes the symbol of the Rebel Alliance.

AWESOME!

Rowan, Zander, and Kordi Freemaker are the first LEGO *Star Wars* minifigures to get their own TV show—LEGO *Star Wars: The Freemaker Adventures.*

TOP 5

Strange species of the LEGO *Star Wars* world with specially crafted heads

1 Mon Calamari (Admiral Ackbar)

2 Ithorian (Jedi Master)

3 Twi'lek (Hera Syndulla)

4 Ewok (Wicket)

5 Um... (Maz Kanata)

Brick History

From 1999 to 2004, most LEGO *Star Wars* minifigures had yellow hands and faces. The first to have a realistic skin tone was Lando Calrissian in 2003.

REALLY?!

In Jabba's Sail Barge (set 75020) R2-D2 is built with an extra piece to turn him into a serving tray!

Q What is the rarest LEGO minifigure?

A That is probably the solid silver C-3PO made to celebrate the 30th anniversary of *Star Wars* in 2007. Only one was ever made, along with five in solid gold.

LOOKS LIKE WE'RE NO LONGER THE NEW GUYS.

Finn

Rey

KEY DATES

1999
The first LEGO® *Star Wars*™ sets include Qui-Gon Jinn, Luke Skywalker, Obi-Wan "Ben" Kenobi, Padmé Amidala, and other heroes.

2008
Sets based on animated TV series *Star Wars: The Clone Wars* follow the adventures of Obi-Wan Kenobi, Anakin Skywalker, and Ahsoka Tano.

2014
A new animated series, *Star Wars Rebels*, spawns LEGO *Star Wars* sets featuring young Ezra Bridger and the crew of the *Ghost*.

2015
Finn and Rey meet old friends Han, Chewie, and Leia as the first LEGO *Star Wars: The Force Awakens* sets are released.

2016
Jyn Erso and a ragtag band of new minifigures try to steal the Death Star plans in LEGO *Star Wars: Rogue One* sets.

Sometimes it's fun to play the bad guy... These minifigure meanies make the LEGO *Star Wars* universe a more exciting place to visit!

Brick History

Since 2011, special minifigures have been given away to mark *Star Wars* Day on May 4. The 2014 minifigure was the mysterious Darth Revan.

FACT STACK

The first LEGO Sith Lord was Darth Maul back in 1999.

Stormtroopers didn't show up in any sets until 2001.

The Jabba the Hutt figure is LEGO *Star Wars*' largest villain.

Jabba's nephew, Rotta the Huttlet, is one of the smallest figures.

ROGER, ROGER, ROGER, ROGER, ROGER, ROGER, ROGER...

147

Battle droid figures found in 54 different LEGO sets.

10,000 limited-edition white Boba Fetts
Based on *Star Wars* concept art and given away in 2010

6 Boba variants with printed faces
Hidden beneath printed visors

5 Boba variants with plain black heads
Visible through helmets with cutaway visors

2 young Bobas
As seen in *Episode II: Attack of the Clones*

1 solid bronze Boba
Awarded to a US competition winner in 2010

AWESOME!
Shiny Captain Phasma is the first minifigure to have a silver blaster. She also has a unique, red-trimmed cape

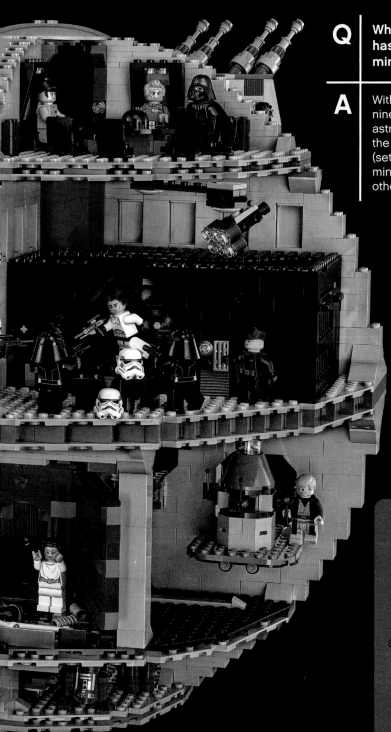

Q Which LEGO set has the most minifigures?

A With 14 Imperials and nine rebels (plus two astromech droids), the 2016 Death Star (set 75159) has more minifigures than any other LEGO set!

I FEEL YOUR PRESENTS.

MOST FESTIVE SITH LORD

Santa Darth Vader (set 75056)

WOW!

The General Grievous figure is made from eight special pieces, none of which is used to make any other character.

IT'S A SIGN!

Get close (but not too close!) to Jabba the Hutt and you'll see the symbol of the Desilijic crime family tattooed on his right arm.

EVIL EYES

Minifigures in sets based on the animated *Star Wars: The Clone Wars* TV show have cartoon-style facial features. This Chancellor Palpatine has striking eyes—no doubt focused on becoming Emperor.

TOP 5 Stylish super troopers

1 Stormtrooper with Orange Pauldron (2012)

2 Red Sith Trooper (2013)

3 Shadow Trooper (2015)

4 Imperial Shock Trooper (2016)

5 Shore Trooper (2016)

Chef (1979)

OOOPS, I DROPPED A BEET.

Fortune Teller (2013)

Janitor (2016)

TV News Reporter (2011)

Admiral (1992)

Rapper (2011)

HEY! THAT'S MY JOB.

ALL WALKS OF LIFE

Air Traffic Controller (1988)

Painter (2011)

Horserider (1986)

King (2004)

Librarian (2013)

Waiter (1990)

Crook (2013)

Firefighter (2015)

Rock Star (2014)

Snake Charmer (2015)

TV Cameraman (1997)

Judge (2013)

DJ (2012)

Coast Guard
(1999)

Sheriff (1996)

Farmer (2009)

Paleontologist (2015)

Evil Mastermind
(2001)

They may be small, but no job is too big for these LEGO minifigures. From kings to crooks, they've got every vacancy filled!

Demolition Worker (2015)

Scientist (1999)

Ninja (2010)

Zookeeper (2011)

Jester (2008)

Soccer Referee (1998)

Wrestler (2010)

Angler (2017)

Stunt Pilot (1993)

WHY WALK WHEN YOU CAN DANCE?

Clown (2010)

Diver (1998)

Carpenter (2015)

LEGO Store
Worker (2015)

Barber (2015)

Ballerina (2016)

Since LEGO® NINJAGO® sets launched in 2011, a team of brave warriors has taken on skeletons, snakes, spooks, Sky Pirates, and more!

FACT STACK

Cole is the Master of Earth. He is a born leader and a great dancer to boot.

Jay is the Master of Lightning. He was the first to master the art of Spinjitzu.

Kai is the Master of Fire. He is the brother of the sixth ninja, Nya.

Nya is the Master of Water. Before becoming a ninja, she was the mysterious Samurai X.

Zane is the Master of Ice. He is a robot and can switch his sense of humor off.

Lloyd is the Green Ninja, foretold by legend. He is also Master Wu's nephew.

LOOK CLOSER

Ever since Zane merged his own mind with the operating system of the android P.I.X.A.L., his visual display has featured the letters "PXL" written backward.

DON'T LOOK NOW BUT THE OTHER PAGE IS FULL OF TERRIBLE VILLAINS.

1,210

Megawatts generated by Jay when he uses his full electrical power.

Zane

Jay

Lloyd

REALLY?!

Before he was an ninja, Lloyd wanted to be a villain. It seemed the obvious choice for the son of evil Lord Garmadon!

Master Wu

Cole

Kai

Nya

Brick History

Kai and Nya's mom and dad were the Elemental Masters of Water and Fire. Nya followed in their mom's footsteps to become the new Master of Water.

▌AWESOME!

Cole was able to walk through walls when Morro the evil Wind Master turned him into a living ghost. ▌

TOP 5

Careers of Ninjago villains before they turned bad

1 **Lord Garmadon:** peaceful teacher.

2 **OverBorg:** brilliant inventor.

3 **Master Chen:** noodle-bar owner.

4 **Morro:** apprentice ninja.

5 **Nadakhan:** pirate (OK, still bad).

Brick History

The Overlord is the oldest villain in the Ninjago world. He was created at the same time as the island itself, and then banished beneath the sea.

IT'S A SIGN!

Nadakhan and his Sky Pirates all wear this scary skull-and-crossed-swords symbol.

General Kozu

TALLEST LEGO MINIFIGURE

General Kozu (set 70504)

Overlord

Nadakhan

Master Chen

Morro

Skulkin

Lord Garmadon

Q | Why did Pythor change color?

A | Pythor used to be purple, but he was bleached white by the stomach acid of a monster that swallowed him. Ugh!

Overborg

Pythor

Prehistoric LEGO beasts

1   **DUPLO** *dinosaurs.* The first LEGO
    dinosaurs lived in LEGO DUPLO
    sets from the late 1990s. More
    preschool than prehistoric, these
    creatures had more chance of
    getting chewed themselves than
    of biting anyone else!

2   *Dino Island.* In 2000, the LEGO
    Adventurers took a trip to
    Dino Island, where Johnny
    Thunder and his fellow explorers
    discovered the blocky footprints
    of tyrannosaurs, triceratops,
    and stegosauruses.

3   *Adaptable dinos.* In 2001, a
    dedicated LEGO® Dinosaurs
    theme featured four-in-one dino
    models such as the aquatic lizard
    Mosasaurus (set 6721), which
    could be rebuilt as an iguanodon,
    a postosuchus, and a dimetrodon.

FOR DINOS

4 **Double Trouble.** The Dino Attack and Dino 2010 themes were launched in 2005, in the US and Europe respectively. The sets had some differences, but shared the same rampaging raptors and a T-rex with light-up eyes.

5 **LEGO Dino.** In 2012, the daring Dino Defense team battled prehistoric beasts in the LEGO® Dino theme. Their quarry included new designs for flying pteranodons, plus a new coelophysis dino with stripes.

6 **LEGO® Jurassic World™.** A colorfully crested Dilophosaurus and an impressive Indominus rex were among the new discoveries when a band of brave minifigures took a trip to LEGO Jurassic World in 2015.

CREATURE FEATURE

Some LEGO animals come fully formed, but these brick beasts are all built to be wild!

Brick History

In 2014, the LEGO Group gave employees a gift set of brick birds native to the UK, China, the USA, Singapore, and Denmark, to celebrate having offices in all those countries.

FACT STACK

One of the first LEGO brick-built animals came in Cowboy & Pony (set 806) in 1964.

The first LEGO Castle knights rode brick-built horses in two 1970s sets.

Fearsome Legend Beasts were among the brick-built creatures in LEGO Legends of Chima.

LEGO® Elves sets feature brick-built dragons similar to the ones in LEGO NINJAGO theme.

WOW!

LEGO® Creator sets such as Red Animals (set 31032) from 2015 can be made into three different animals—in this case a dragon, a snake, and a scorpion.

REALLY?!

Feed the hungry parrot in LEGO Creator Rainforest Animals (set 31031) from 2015 and his food literally passes right through him!

TOP 5 — LEGO NINJAGO dragons

1 The **Fusion Dragon** has the powers of both its riders—Fire ninja Kai and Water ninja Nya.

2 The ghostly **Morro Dragon** was the first NINJAGO dragon to have fabric wings.

3 The **Green NRG Dragon** soars through the sky with a wingspan of 22in (57cm).

4 Lloyd's **Golden Dragon** has a molded head piece, like all NINJAGO dragons released before 2014.

Piece particulars

Deep Sea Predators (set 4506) from 2004 used rare glow-in-the-dark pieces to make fearsome fish teeth and spooky squid bits!

WOW!

Far from prehistoric, the 2008 LEGO Creator Stegosaurus (set 4998) contains a light-up brick to create glowing eyes.

AWESOME!

In 2010 and 2011, LEGO® Atlantis sets pitted minifigure divers against brick-built sea creatures, including an angry angler fish!

MINI BEASTS

Every month, LEGO stores around the world hold Mini Model Builds, where fans can make and keep a free LEGO model. In 2017, the builds included unusual animals like narwhals and platypuses.

2

Number of pieces needed to make a LEGO fly—like the one on the tongue of this LEGO Creator Chameleon (set 30477) from 2017!

5
The mighty four-headed **Ultra Dragon** is four Elemental Dragons combined into one force!

CHARACTER BUILDING

LEGO figures don't have to be mini! From purely brick-built characters to articulated action figures, there are many ways to build a big personality.

FACT STACK

The first brick-built characters could not be posed and had no jointed or moving parts.

Today's buildable characters use parts other than bricks to allow for realistic movement.

Modern buildable figures are designed to be as robust in play as normal action figures.

There have been more buildable models of Santa Claus than any other character!

HO! HO! HO!

Piece particulars

LEGO ball-and-socket joints were introduced in 1970 for connections such as vehicle tow bars. Most buildable figures are made with newer ball-and-socket friction joints, which connect more tightly for poseability.

REALLY?!

Looking good enough to eat, Birthday Buddy (set 40226) is a brick-built cupcake character released in 2016.

FRESH FACES

In 1974, the first LEGO figures with printed faces and articulated arms were released. Now known as "maxifigures" by fans, they had torsos and legs built from standard bricks, and appeared in more than 30 sets.

Q | What is the Character and Creature Building System (CCBS)?

A | CCBS is the LEGO Group's name for a figure-building system that was introduced in 2011. It features jointed "skeleton" parts and snap-on "shell" pieces that can create large, articulated characters and creatures.

TOP 5

Cool parts used in LEGO Mixels

1 **Volectro** has hair made out of a bush.

2 **Slumbo** has minifigure helmets for eyelids.

3 **Turg** has a tail piece for a tongue.

4 **Forx** has banana pieces for eyebrows.

5 **Dribbal** has a crystal piece as his... Ugh!

BRICK CHALLENGE

Build a model of yourself out of LEGO bricks. Can you make it move using joints or hinge pieces?

KEY DATES

1999
The LEGO Technic Slizer subtheme (also known as Throwbots) introduces buildable figures articulated using large ball-and-socket friction connectors.

2001
The first BIONICLE buildable figures blend LEGO Technic articulation with unique, characterful mask pieces and a detailed storyline.

2011
LEGO® Hero Factory introduces a new buildable figure system, still based on ball-and-socket joints, but easier to build and stronger in play.

2015
After a four-year break, LEGO® BIONICLE® returns to stores with sturdy new figures based on the LEGO Hero Factory building system.

HAS ANYONE GOT A TISSUE?

13
Points of articulation on Burnzie from LEGO NEXO KNIGHTS Axl's Tower Carrier (set 70322).

ODDEST BRICK-BUILT CHARACTERS
Clowns (set 321)

WOW!
Characters that exist as minifigures and large buildable figures include Batman, Buzz Lightyear, Spongebob Squarepants, and Laval from LEGO Legends of Chima.

Brick History

In 1963, the US-only Doll Set (set 905) included more than 200 pieces for building a pirate captain, ballet dancers, a musician, a coachman, and more.

GO SPORTS!

In a world where croissants are the size of your arm, LEGO minifigures need to stay in shape. Luckily for them, there's a healthy array of sports-themed sets.

FACT STACK

LEGO minifigures can play more than 25 sports, including pool in the Detective's Office (set 10246, pictured).

One of the rarest minifigures ever made was a 1999 Boston Red Sox baseball player.

The 2003 LEGO® Sports theme featured minifigure basketball players with spring-loaded legs.

In LEGO® Friends, Stephanie is a keen soccer player and Mia is an award-winning horse rider.

I CHEER WHEN THERE'S A GHOUL!

REALLY?!

The LEGO Minifigures theme has featured three different cheerleaders, with the latest being a Zombie Cheerleader.

7

Cyclist minifigures in 2000's Telekom Race Cyclists and Winners' Podium (set 1199)—but only one winner in a yellow jersey!

Brick History

In 2016, the German soccer team were turned into a LEGO Minifigures series. Fifteen players came with soccer balls, while manager Joachim Löw came with a unique tactics board.

BUILT ON ICE

Between 2003 and 2004, LEGO® Sports Hockey sets featured minifigures, small figures built from LEGO Technic elements, and larger, BIONICLE style figures with powerful puck-hitting mechanisms!

AWESOME!

In 2003, LEGO Sports Gravity Games featured daredevil skateboarder and snowboarder minifigures who could be sent speeding down special ramp pieces.

I BETTER GET THIS SHOT NOW EVERYONE IS WATCHING.

YOU CAN DO IT, CHAMP!

Piece particulars

The Boxer from 2011 was the first minifigure not to have at least one standard hand piece. His gloves attach straight onto his arms!

COMES-WITH-AN-ACTUAL-MEDAL WINNER

Swimming Champion

WOW!

In 2000, LEGO® Soccer (also known as LEGO Football) used tilting, turning minifigure bases so that players could aim and kick.

IT'S A SIGN!

In 2001, Women's Team (set 3416) featured six female soccer players, plus stickers to kit them out in American, Canadian, Brazilian, or Mexican jerseys.

TOP 5
Collectible competitors

1 Downhil Skier (Series 8, 2012)

2 Sumo Wrestler (Series 3, 2011)

3 Tennis Ace (Series 7, 2012)

4 Roller Derby Girl (Series 9, 2013)

5 Fencer (Series 13, 2015)

Top 5

Most brick-chilling collectibles

1. **Banshee** (series 14, 2015)
2. **Zombie Businessman** (series 14, 2015)
3. **Spectre** (series 14, 2015)
4. **Medusa** (series 10, 2013)
5. **Fly Monster** (series 14, 2015)

Banshee

Zombie Businessman

IT'S A SIGN!

The Zombie Pirate Captain's hat has an even creepier skull-and-crossbones design than regular LEGO pirates.

ZOMBIE TIMES

BRAAAIN

Fly Monster

Spectre

Medusa

13

Number of sets released in the LEGO® Monster Fighters theme in 2012.

Brick History

LEGO vampires first appeared in LEGO® Studios sets in 2002. Since then, more vampires have emerged from the shadows in LEGO Minifigures, LEGO® Games, and LEGO Monster Fighters sets.

Piece particulars

The LEGO Minifigures Monster from 2011 has a special head extension, stitched up to keep his brain in place. This spooky part has been used in different creepy colors for Monster Rocker (pictured) and Monster Butler minifigures.

Q What do LEGO monsters do in their spare time?

A They chill! The Monster Butler in 2012's Haunted House (set 10228) likes to dance to music. His mummy friends got him into rapping.

ARRGH!

White head pieces with spooky skull designs appear in more than 70 sets—and not always with bodies to rest on!

LOOK CLOSER

The Werewolf minifigure wears the same shirt as the Lumberjack. One unlucky night in the woods and the poor Lumberjack was transformed, howling at the Moon!

BOO!

In 1990, the ghost shroud was the first glow-in-the-dark LEGO element. Glowing ghosts have since appeared in 16 scary sets.

MINI MONSTERS

Did you know that the LEGO world has a darker side? These ghouls and monsters make LEGO sets go bump in the night and will get your teeth chattering!

Special scale LEGO figures

1 DUPLO *dolls.* Four large LEGO DUPLO dolls with realistic proportions and fabric clothes were released in 2001. Standing about 18 bricks high, each doll came with its own, much smaller, doll toy that was slightly larger than a LEGO minifigure.

2 SCALA *dolls.* The largest and most realistic of all LEGO figures, LEGO® SCALA dolls stood more than 6in (15.2cm) tall, wore fabric clothes, and had brushable hair. The dolls featured in more than 40 sets between 1997 and 2001.

3 LEGO Technic *figures.* The first LEGO Technic figures braved the cold in Arctic-themed sets from 1986. Looking like taller, more athletic minifigures, they appeared in 36 sets in 28 variations—including scary cyborgs!

4 BELVILLE *figures.* Twice the height of a minifigure, each BELVILLE figure had 14 points of articulation— more than any other LEGO figure. Launched in 1994, the theme also included baby figures and, later, small fairies without any articulation.

ALL SHAPES AND SIZES

5 **FABULAND** *figures*. More than 20 animal species inhabited the FABULAND world between 1979 and 1989. They all shared the same articulated body shape and included crocodiles, hippos, and walruses.

6 **DUPLO** *figures*. In 1977, the first LEGO DUPLO figures had chunky single-block bodies and heads that turned but didn't come off. By 1983, some DUPLO figures had moving arms and legs, but still no removable parts for safety reasons.

7 *Basic figures.* LEGO Basic figures came in two variations between 1981 and 1991: blue and red. Their hollow bodies meant they could be used as finger puppets, and they were the first LEGO figures to have noses!

FACTION PACKED

I WENT GREEN BEFORE IT WAS FASHIONABLE!

Since 1978, more than 20 different factions have battled for supremacy in the LEGO Castle theme, from King's Knights to outlaws and even trolls!

14

Knights in 1978's Castle (set 375)—the most minifigures in any 20th-century set.

HAIR TO THE THRONE

For the first 20 years of LEGO Castle, only four minifigures had hair pieces instead of helmets. The first were nobles in Knight's Joust (set 383) from 1979.

SHIELDS UP!

LEGO Castle knights have fought with more than 40 different shields since 1978. Here are just a few from over the years.

Crusaders (1984)   **Black Falcons** (1984)   **Forestmen** (1988)   **Dragon Knights** (1993)   **Royal Knights** (1995)   **Lion Knights** (2000)   **Shadow Knights** (2005)

AWESOME!

In 2004, LEGO® KNIGHTS' KINGDOM™ characters could be collected in minifigure form or as big, buildable action figures.

TOP 5
LEGO Castle fantasy figures

1 **Ghost,** in sets from 1990.

2 **Skeleton,** in sets from 1995.

3 **Dwarf,** in sets from 2007.

4 **Troll,** in sets from 2008.

5 **Giant Troll,** in sets from 2008.

FOR ONE KNIGHT ONLY!

WOW!

A 2016 LEGO.com exclusive (set 5004419) featured a 1980s-style knight and a LEGO knights timeline in a special presentation box.

MOST BLING KING
Crown King (set 7078)

IT'S A SIGN!

The first LEGO Castle knights from 1978 came with a sheet of stickers to decorate their plain gray tabard and shield pieces.

Brick History

In 1993, the Dragon Masters became the first minifigures in any theme to have mismatched arms and legs—a style later taken up by LEGO Castle jesters.

I'M A GOOD GUY, REALLY!

Q Who are the bad guys in early LEGO Castle sets?

A That's entirely up to you! It was not until the 1990s that villainous factions such as the Wolfpack appeared in LEGO Castle sets.

Skeleton Warriors (2007)

Troll Warriors (2007)

King's Knights (2013)

MODERN KNIGHTS

Meet the minifigure citizens of the NEXO KNIGHTS kingdom; from the heroes that fight to defend it, to the monsters who want to destroy it!

Brick History

The wizard Merlok 2.0 appears as a printed piece in sets because he was blasted into a computer system and became a hologram. The only minifigure of the human Merlok is included with DK's *The Book of Knights* (2016).

FACT STACK

Clay Moorington is determined to become the greatest knight ever. His emblem is the falcon.

Aaron Fox is a reckless daredevil and a great archer. His emblem is the fox.

Lance Richmond is a celebrity knight who is not as brave as his fans think! His emblem is the horse.

Axl is big and strong—probably because he eats so much! His emblem is the bull.

Macy Halbert is a princess but her true calling is knighthood! Her emblem is the dragon.

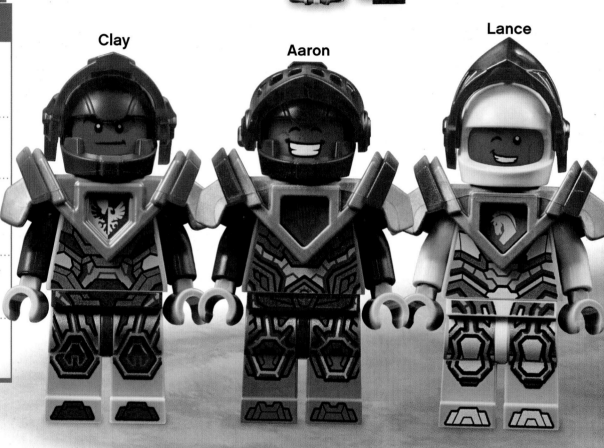

Clay

Aaron

Lance

IT'S A SIGN!

In Aaron's Stone Destroyer (set 70358), Robot Hoodlum the rebel squirebot wears the same stag emblem as the LEGO Castle Forestmen.

WHAT'S A BOT?

While the NEXO KNIGHTS heroes are busy saving the realm, lots of everyday jobs in Knighton are done by mechanical bots. Chef Eclair is the King's chefbot, and each knight has a faithful squirebot to help them out.

Q Who is the bad guy in the LEGO NEXO KNIGHTS world?

A Jestro, the King's former jester, is the theme's main villain. The Book of Monsters tricked him into turning bad and now he kind of likes it!

AWESOME!

Knight-in-training Robin Underwood hasn't graduated from the Knight's Academy yet, but he still goes undercover as the mysterious Black Knight.

Piece particulars

The Book of Monsters is made up of two pieces that were first introduced in NEXO KNIGHTS sets: a book "plate" and a hinged book cover.

OPEN ME UP, I DARE YA!

Axl

Macy

ROYAL RELATIONS

King and Queen Halbert are the kindly rulers of Knighton. Macy is their daughter. She has more in common with her courageous mom than her easily frightened father!

LAVA MONSTERS

MADE FROM	Molten-hot lava
SKILLS	Shooting fire, burning knights
LEADER	General Magmar
RANKS	Flame Throwers, Scurriers, Globlins
MONSTER FACT	Lavaria is the Lava army's sneaky spy

STONE MONSTERS

MADE FROM	Super-hard rock
SKILLS	Crushing things, blasting electricity
LEADER	General Garg
RANKS	Stone Stompers, Gargoyles, Bricksters
MONSTER FACT	They were rocks and statues before lightning brought them to life

VS.

SMALL BUT MIGHTY

Heroes come in all shapes and sizes, but in the world of LEGO® DC Super Heroes, they are all approximately four bricks high!

Q | What is LEGO Robin's true identity?

A | There have been several LEGO Robins, including Tim Drake (also known as "Red Robin"), Dick Grayson, and Damian Wayne. But keep that under your cape!

Brick History

Though the first LEGO DC Super Heroes sets were not released until 2012, exclusive Batman, Superman, and Green Lantern minifigures were given away at special events in 2011.

FACT STACK

There are more than 130 LEGO DC Super Heroes minifigures.

More than 60 minifigures in the theme fight on the side of truth and justice.

The assorted heroes include more than 20 Batman variations.

Superman and other Kryptonians appear in over a dozen sets.

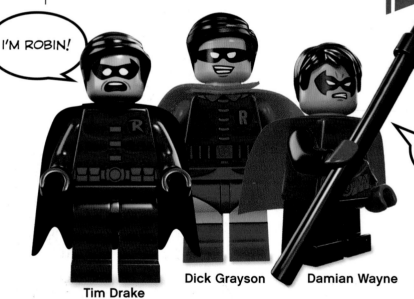

I'M ROBIN!

NO, I'M ROBIN!

Tim Drake

Dick Grayson

Damian Wayne

LOOK INTO MY EYES...

LITTLE WONDER

There have been four different Wonder Woman minifigures, but only the Mighty Micros version comes with short legs.

9

LEGO themes in which Batman appears: LEGO Batman, LEGO BrickHeadz, LEGO DC Super Heroes, LEGO® DIMENSIONS™, LEGO DUPLO, LEGO Juniors, LEGO Minifigures, THE LEGO® BATMAN MOVIE™, and THE LEGO MOVIE!

▌AWESOME!

Armored Batman from Clash of the Heroes (set 76044) is the only LEGO DC Super Heroes minifigure with glow-in-the-dark eyes!

SCARIEST-
LOOKING
GOOD GUY

Cyborg from
Darkseid Invasion
(set 76028)

TOP 5
Lesser-known heroes

1 Plastic Man
(set 5004081)

2 Beast Boy
(set 76035)

3 Hawkman
(set 76028)

4 Blue Beetle
(set 76054)

5 Katana
(set 76055)

LOOK CLOSER

Part of an exclusive 2015 gift cube
(set 5004077), the rare Lightning Lad
minifigure has lightning-bolt eyebrows!

IT'S A SIGN!

Superman's "S-Shield"
is actually a Kryptonian
family crest. It is also
worn by his father, Jor-El,
and his cousin, Kara, also
known as Supergirl.

BUILT TO BE BAD

Super Heroes are nothing without their enemies. This Rogues Gallery causes chaos for the good guys in LEGO DC Super Heroes sets.

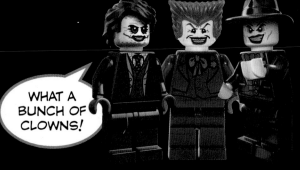

WHAT A BUNCH OF CLOWNS!

LOOK CLOSER

In Batman: Rescue from Rā's al Ghūl (set 76056), anti-hero Talia al Ghūl has carved "B+T" (Batman and Talia) in a heart shape on the wall of a hideout.

The Joker

The Riddler

MOST BADLY DRESSED BADDIE

Trickster

CALL ME "LOCKS LUTHOR"!

REALLY?!

Lex Luthor battles Superman in three sets, but only in Heroes of Justice: Sky-High Battle (set 76046) does he have any hair.

THE JOKER'S WILD!

The Joker isn't just a minifigure. In 2012, he was one of four LEGO DC Super Heroes Buildable Figures (set 4527), and in 2017 he was one of the first LEGO BrickHeadz models (set 41588).

LOOK CLOSER

Harleen Quinzel might look like a friendly doctor, but under her white coat you can see the red and black outfit of villainous Harley Quinn!

WOW!

Green Lantern's alien enemy Sinestro is the only minifigure ever to have a bright purple head!

NO, I'M NOT HOLDING MY BREATH.

The Penguin

Mr. Freeze

Catwoman

REALLY?!

Black Manta is an undersea enemy of Aquaman who seeks to control the oceans using laser-shooting cyborg sharks.

IT'S A SIGN!

Batzarro is a mixed-up monster version of Batman, created by Lex Luthor. He wears the Caped Crusader's famous symbol on his chest but, like his Utility Belt, it is upside-down.

Bad guys so big they don't fit into minifigure form: Gorilla Grodd, Killer Croc, and Darkseid!

Stars of the DC Super Hero Girls theme

1 **Harley Quinn.** She might be the class clown, but Harley is also a brilliant brain and an agile gymnast. She pilots a jet plane (set 41231).

2 **Wonder Woman.** She has a Lasso of Truth that stops others from telling lies. This hero also has an invisible bike in Wonder Woman Dorm Room (set 41235).

3 **Supergirl.** Superman's cousin is the most powerful teen on the planet. Instead of a vehicle, she uses her ace flying skills to catch the bad guys.

4 **Batgirl.** She is a tech genius as well as a determined crime-fighter. Batgirl flies a Batjet (set 41230) with net and stud shooters.

5 **Bumblebee.** This hero can fly like a real bee and has electric-blast sting powers. Her Bumblebee Helicopter (set 41234) helps her see off troublemakers.

6 **Poison Ivy.** A biology expert with a passion for plant life, Poison Ivy drives a plant-shooting green motorbike (set 41232).

7 **Lashina.** This young warrior is known for her whip-cracking skills. She drives a tough tank (set 41233).

8 **Super Hero High School.** The girls' school (set 41232) transforms into battle mode when attacked, with a ramp that lowers from the tower and a rooftop shooter.

POWER!

CHAPTER FIVE

BEYOND
THE BRICK

The LEGO Group was founded by master carpenter and joiner Ole Kirk Kristiansen.

Ole Kirk ran the company until 1957, when his son, Godtfred Kirk Christiansen, took over.

In 1979, Ole Kirk's grandson, Kjeld Kirk Kristiansen, was made chief executive officer.

Today, the LEGO Group is jointly owned by Kjeld Kirk and his three children.

WOW!

Ole Kirk Kristiansen came up with the LEGO name by combining the Danish words "leg godt" meaning "play well."

Ole, Godtfred, and Kjeld Kirk Kristiansen together in 1951.

KEY DATES

1891
Ole Kirk Kristiansen is born in Omvrå, in the Blaahøj-Filskov region of Denmark (not far from Billund), on April 7.

1903
Ole Kirk becomes an apprentice carpenter and joiner, learning skills from his brother Kristian Bonde Kristiansen in Give, Denmark.

1916
After completing his apprenticeship and military service, Ole Kirk buys a joinery factory in the rural community of Billund.

1924
Wood shavings in Ole Kirk's workshop catch fire, causing the workshop and the family home to burn down. Work starts on rebuilding a new house (pictured).

1932
A global economic crisis threatens Ole Kirk's rebuilt business. With no other carpentry work available, he begins to make wooden toys.

1934
Ole Kirk holds a competition among his employees to name his growing company. He wins it himself by devising the LEGO name!

Q Why are Ole Kirk Kristiansen and Godtfred Kirk Christiansen's surnames spelled differently?

A Both were born "Kristiansen," but it was common to use both spellings interchangeably. Ole Kirk used both versions, but kept "Kristiansen" on his birth certificate, while Godtfred officially changed to the "Ch" spelling in the 1980s.

The house and workshop Ole Kirk Kristiansen built in 1924 still stands in Billund, and has even been made into a LEGO set.

IT'S A SIGN!

DET-BEDSTE-ER IKKE-FOR-GODT

When Ole Kirk Kristiansen coined the LEGO Group motto "Only the best is good enough" in 1936, his son Godtfred Kirk Christiansen turned it into a woodcut for the wall of their workshop.

REALLY?!

In its early days as a wooden toy manufacturer, the LEGO Group also made ladders and ironing boards!

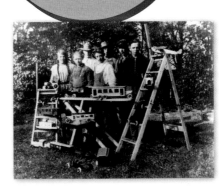

10

The number of employees who worked at the LEGO factory in 1939.

PLASTIC PIONEER

Ole Kirk Kristiansen was among the first to see the potential of plastic toys. An early success was a model tractor in 1952. Though expensive to make, the tractor turned a healthy profit, which helped him to further develop another product: plastic bricks.

WHERE IT ALL BEGAN

The worldwide success of the LEGO Group can all be traced back to one man in a workshop in Billund, Denmark, where the company still has its headquarters today.

BRICK BEGINNINGS

LEGO® bricks get to be spaceships, sports cars, castles, and more—but there's another amazing journey they all go on first!

1 LEGO bricks start out as small plastic granules called granulate, each one smaller than a grain of rice. The Billund factory, Kornmarken, can get through 110 tons (100 tonnes) of granulate in a single day.

2 Powerful vacuum pumps suck the granulate out of huge metal silos and whizz it through pipes into molding machines. Every factory has many miles of pipes and several hundred molding machines.

3 When it reaches the machinery, the granulate is melted into a thick, gooey liquid at temperatures ranging from 446°F to 590°F (230°C to 310°C)—that's up to three times hotter than boiling water.

4 The liquid plastic is injected into a metal mold and instantly starts to cool. To make sure it forms a perfect brick, it is subjected to pressure of up to 14.5 tons per square inch (2 tonnes per cm²).

5 Bricks harden in around 10 to 15 seconds, after which they are ejected from the molds. They fall onto a conveyor belt and into large crates, then some from each batch are taken for testing.

6 During quality testing, bricks are measured to within the width of a human hair (0.0002in, or 0.004mm) to make sure they fit together perfectly and have just the right amount of what the LEGO Group refers to as "clutch power."

7 When a crate of bricks is full, a robot truck collects it, labels it with a unique code, and sends it to be stored. In the huge Kornmarken warehouse, crates can be stacked up to 65ft (20m) high.

8 When a crate is needed, a robot crane knows exactly where it is! It confirms what's inside using the unique label, slides the crate out of the stack, and sends it on its way along a conveyor belt.

15 Robot cranes load the packaged sets onto pallets for distribution by road and by sea. Bricks that were piles of granulate just a short time ago are now on their way to stores and homes around the world!

9 If the bricks in the crate need a printed design on them, such as the vests on these LEGO City Police minifigure torsos, they are sent to the decoration department.

14 The plastic bags pass down chutes and are placed in the cardboard display boxes they will be sold in. The boxes are checked and sealed by machine, then sealed into larger boxes for delivery.

10 Some parts are put together in the factory, including minifigure legs onto hips and wheels onto tires. These parts go through their own special assembly machines before they rejoin the main production line.

13 High-precision scales weigh the boxes along the route to make sure no pieces are missing. At the end of the conveyor belt, another machine seals the contents of each small box inside a plastic bag.

11 After any printing and assembly, all bricks arrive in the packing department. They are loaded into machines that eject the bricks one at a time, or in the numbers needed for a specific set.

12 Bricks of different kinds meet for the first time as small boxes pass beneath the packing machines, filling up with the precise selection of parts required as they go along.

BOX CLEVER

Q | Do all LEGO sets come in boxes?

A | No, not all. There have also been LEGO® BIONICLE® carry canisters, LEGO brick-shaped creative building tubs, and LEGO® DUPLO® sets shaped like everything from airplanes to animals.

The LEGO Group gives its boxes, bags, and tubs the same care and attention that it gives to the LEGO bricks and models inside the packaging.

WOW!

Since June 2014, standard LEGO products have been sold in more environmentally friendly boxes, made from materials certified by the Forest Stewardship Council®.

REALLY?!

In 2008, Kjeld Kirk Kristiansen reprised his role as a LEGO box star for Town Plan (set 10184), celebrating 50 years of the LEGO brick. By this point, Kjeld Kirk was also the owner of the LEGO Group.

LOOK CLOSER

Several LEGO set boxes of the 1950s featured LEGO Group founder Ole Kirk Kristiansen's grandchildren, Hanne, Gunhild, and Kjeld Kirk, playing with the bricks inside.

Brick History

Between 1956 and 1959, the front of LEGO Town Plan boxes featured paintings of the sets inside, along with a friendly figure usually known as the LEGO Gnome.

REALLY?!

From 1957 to 1972, some LEGO sets came in large wooden boxes. They are now collector's items—even when they don't have any LEGO bricks in them!

All modern LEGO sets have a picture of a life-size LEGO brick or minifigure somewhere on the packaging, just in case anyone has never seen a real LEGO brick before!

10,004

Number of pieces contained in the biggest-ever LEGO box. The Ultimate Battle For CHIMA contained 25 LEGO® Legends of Chima™ sets and was the grand prize in a 2015 LEGO Club competition.

LEGO LEGENDS OF CHIMA™

Ages/edades 9+
The ultimate battle for CHIMA
10004 pcs/Stck/pzs/db
Building Toy
Konstruktionsspielzeug
Jouet de construction
Juguete para Construir
Brinquedo para Construir
Építőjáték

I MADE THIS

LEGO Designers put their all into making new sets, so it's no surprise that they sometimes include personal references and nods to their favorite old sets.

Dizzy heights. The nervous-looking minifigure in 2015's LEGO Creator Expert Ferris Wheel (set 10247) is a joke about Set Designer Jamie Berard's reluctance to ride on the real thing!

Why is she waiting? The LEGO Minifigures Diner Waitress from 2013 is based on LEGO Designer Tara Wike, and she wears a name badge to prove it.

Written in the stars. Stickers in 2011's LEGO Space Earth Defense HQ (set 7066) are Set Designer Mark Stafford's tribute to the late Nate Nielsen, a LEGO fan builder known online as "Nnenn."

On the map. The "LEGO Town" map in 2008's 50th anniversary LEGO set, Town Plan (set 10184), actually shows where the LEGO Group was founded in Billund, Denmark.

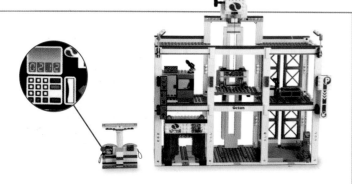

It's a date! The price of gas shown in 2012's City Garage (set 4207) from the LEGO City theme just happens to be the birth date of Designer Samuel Johnson.

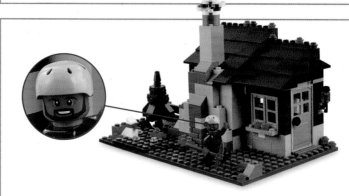

Smiling selfie. The bearded trail biker in the LEGO Creator Mountain Hut (set 31025) from 2014 is a minifigure self-portrait by Set Designer Morten Rauff.

Face of the farm. The farmer in 2009's LEGO City Farm subtheme is based on LEGO Designer Chris Bonveen. When Chris himself came to design a new farmer in 2016, he used the opportunity to show how he had aged in real life!

A familiar face. Designer Matthew Boyle based the banker's portrait in 2016's LEGO Creator Expert Brick Bank (set 10251) on Chris Bonveen (see left). He reasoned that it was a picture of the minifigure farmer's brother!

Pet project. Glurt (set 41519) from 2014's LEGO® Mixels™ range is based on LEGO Set Designer Mark Stafford's dog—only green and much more slimy.

Family affair. Set Designer Jamie Berard based a minifigure in 2009's Winter Toy Shop (set 10199) on his mom, and named Chez Albert in 2014's Parisian Restaurant (set 10243) after his dad.

DUPLO D.O.B. Senior Designer Mette Grue-Sørensen used license plates to personalize her designs. The cars at 2009's LEGO DUPLO Petrol Station (set 5640) and Busy Garage (set 5641) all have her initials and date of birth on the back.

Train tribute. The flight numbers listed on the departure board in 1990's LEGO Town Airport Shuttle (set 6399) are, in fact, set numbers of classic 1980s LEGO Trains.

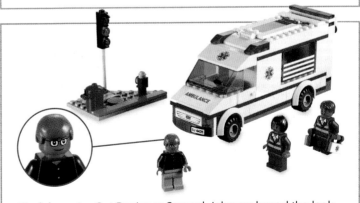

Model mentor. Set Designer Samuel Johnson based the look of the cyclist minifigure in 2012's LEGO City Ambulance (set 4431) on his mentor, LEGO Master Model Coach Torben Skov.

WOW!

At the world's largest LEGO Store in Leicester Square, London, the LEGO Mosaic Maker will turn your photo into a personalized LEGO portrait.

LEGO
10+
40179

250,000

People are expected to visit the new LEGO® House in Billund, Denmark every year.

TOP 5

Models at the LEGO Store in Leicester Square, London

1 LEGO Big Ben stands over 21ft (6.5m) tall and chimes every hour.

2 This LEGO London Underground train is the biggest model in the store.

A WORLD OF DISCOVERY

LEGOLAND® Discovery Centers are indoor attractions with rides, building areas, 4-D cinema shows, and more. There are Discovery Centers in Germany, Turkey, the UK, China, Japan, Canada, and Australia—plus nine in the USA alone.

Q What is the LEGO House?

A The LEGO House is a new way to discover the LEGO story in the home of the LEGO brick. The three-acre (12,000m²) building in Billund, Denmark is packed full of fun things to see and do, spread across six different interactive zones.

LOOK CLOSER

The "Keystone" on top of the LEGO House in Billund, Denmark is shaped like a giant 2x4 LEGO brick.

3 Store mascot, **Lester,** is built from 24,500 bricks.

4 This **LEGO telephone box** weighs more than 1,500lbs (700kg).

5 **Brickley the Dragon** took 725 hours to build.

The LEGO Group sometimes makes micro-scale models of its factories, such as Kladno Campus in the Czech Republic, as gifts for staff.

Brick History

In 1974, the first LEGO factory outside Denmark opened in Switzerland. Today, LEGO bricks are produced in factories in Denmark, Hungary, Mexico, the Czech Republic, and China.

Brick statistics

The LEGO factory in Jiaxing, China

20 football fields
Would fit inside the 40-acre (165,000m²) factory

1,200+ employees
Worked at the factory in 2016

20,000 solar panels
Provide green energy for the factory

400,000 LEGO boxes
Can be stored in the factory warehouse

FACT STACK

There are more than 130 LEGO Brand Retail Stores in 10 countries around the world.

LEGO Group HQ is still based in Billund, Denmark, where the company was founded.

Every LEGO office around the world is stocked with bowls of bricks for staff to play with!

People from more than 30 countries work at LEGO HQ in Billund, Denmark.

REALLY?!

Every year, a few lucky fans get to see inside the LEGO factory in Billund, Denmark, as part of the LEGO Inside Tour.

COME ON IN

Not all LEGO buildings are made from plastic bricks! There are also the factories, stores, offices, and visitor centers found in various locations around the world.

IT'S A LEGOLAND® WORLD!

The first LEGOLAND® park opened in Billund, Denmark, in 1968. Less than 50 years later, there are now eight LEGOLAND destinations in three continents.

WOW!

The 4-D movie theaters at LEGOLAND parks can feature live wind, water, and smoke effects to bring the action on screen to life!

TOP 5

LEGOLAND rollercoasters

1 Polar X-plorer at LEGOLAND Billund
Height: 62ft (18.8m)
Speed: 40mph (65kmph)

2 The Dragon at LEGOLAND Deutschland and Dubai
Height: 53ft (16m)
Speed: 37mph (60kmph)

3 LEGO® Technic Rollercoaster at LEGOLAND California
Height: 52ft (15.8m)
Speed: 35mph (56kmph)

4 Flying School at LEGOLAND Florida
Height: 48ft (14.6m)
Speed: 26mph (42kmph)

5 The Dragon at LEGOLAND Windsor
Height: 34ft (10.3m)
Speed: 30mph (48kmph)

LEGOLAND FLORIDA
United States, opened 2011

Incorporates a botanical garden that has stood on the site since 1936.

LEGOLAND CALIFORNIA
United States, opened 1999

Home to the world's first LEGOLAND Water Park.

THE LEGO GLOBE

The eight LEGOLAND parks are spread around the world, each with something special to see.

BRICK CHALLENGE
Can you design a new LEGOLAND ride using your own LEGO bricks?

AWESOME!

Many rooms in LEGOLAND hotels contain a locked safe with LEGO treasures inside—and clues for cracking the code!

REALLY?!

The original Traffic School cars in LEGOLAND Billund ran from 1968 to 2015 before they needed to be replaced.

55,000,000+

Visitors to LEGOLAND Billund since it opened in 1968.

Brick statistics

LEGO® NINJAGO® World at LEGOLAND Billund

727,000 LEGO bricks
Used to build the attraction in 2016

400ft (122m) of track
Winding through LEGO NINJAGO: The Ride

42ft (13m) across
Size of the largest 3-D display in the attraction

30 laser beams
To dodge in Lloyd's Laser Maze

LEGOLAND DEUTSCHLAND
Germany, opened 2002

See it all from the 164ft (50m) observation tower.

LEGOLAND BILLUND
Denmark, opened 1968

The first LEGOLAND has trebled in size since it opened.

LEGOLAND JAPAN
Japan, opened 2017

A day at this park starts with a LEGO factory tour.

LEGOLAND WINDSOR
United Kingdom, opened 1996

Built with more than 80 million LEGO bricks.

LEGOLAND DUBAI
United Arab Emirates, opened 2016

The only LEGOLAND Resort with an indoor MINILAND.

LEGOLAND MALAYSIA
Malaysia, opened 2012

The first LEGOLAND Resort to open in Asia.

FAN-TASTIC IDEAS

Thanks to the LEGO® Ideas theme, LEGO fan builders can now see their coolest creations turned into official LEGO sets for everyone to enjoy!

Brick History

Daniel Siskind was the first LEGO fan to have his idea turned into an official set: the LEGO My Own Creation Blacksmith Shop (set 3739), back in 2002.

IT'S A SIGN!

No new parts are created for LEGO Ideas sets, but new prints are used to decorate existing pieces—such as the stylish stripes and sevens on 2016's Caterham Seven 620R (set 21307).

FACT STACK

LEGO Ideas started out as LEGO CUUSOO, a website for LEGO fans in Japan, in 2008.

"Cuusoo" is a Japanese word meaning "imagination" and can also mean "wish."

LEGO CUUSOO launched around the world in 2011 and became LEGO Ideas in 2014.

More than 20,000 fan-designed projects have been submitted to the LEGO Ideas website.

Colibri thalassinus

I'M A BIG LEGO FAN MADE SMALL.

STAR NAMES

Fan builder Peter Reid hasn't just designed a LEGO Ideas set—he's been turned into a minifigure! The two astronauts in his Exo Suit (set 21109) from 2014 are called Pete and Yve, after him and his girlfriend, Yvonne Doyle.

Q | How do I submit an idea for a new LEGO set?

A | If you are aged 13 or older, you can create a LEGO Ideas profile, submit your own ideas, and support others at ideas.LEGO.com.

❙ AWESOME!

Fan builder Thomas Poulsom has designed 40 LEGO birds as well as the three that feature in his 2015 LEGO Ideas set, Birds (set 21301).

The LEGO Ideas Maze (set 21305) from 2016 is a mechanical ball game with tip-and-tilt controls. The set comes with ideas for customizing the maze design.

LARGEST LEGO IDEAS SET

Old Fishing Store (set 21309)

POLICE PUBLIC CALL BOX

POLICE PUBLIC CALL BOX

Andrew Clark, the fan designer behind Doctor Who (set 21304), is the nephew of Paul McGann—the eighth actor to play the Doctor in the BBC sci-fi series.

ROLE-MODEL MAKING

LEGO fan builder Ellen Kooijman designed 2014's Research Institute (set 21110) to inspire girls to become anything they want to be—including paleontologists, chemists, and astronomers.

Cyanocitta cristata

rithacus becula

10,000

The number of supporters a project needs before being considered by the LEGO Review Board as a possible set.

MOST FORGETFUL MINIFIGURE

Where Are My Pants? Guy

OH, HERE THEY ARE!

In 2014, THE LEGO® MOVIE™ proved that everything is AWESOME!!! A sequel to THE LEGO MOVIE is expected to arrive in theaters early in 2019. Even more AWESOME!!!

4

Different versions of the infectious theme song Everything is AWESOME!!! feature on THE LEGO MOVIE soundtrack. AWESOME!!!

FACT STACK

THE LEGO MOVIE hit US theaters on February 7, 2014, and became one of the biggest animated movies of the year.

Everything you see in THE LEGO MOVIE was built using digital versions of real LEGO bricks.

Animators added scratches, teeth-marks, and fingerprints to make the minifigures look like authentic toys.

More than 20 sets were released based on THE LEGO MOVIE including Super Cycle Chase (set 70808, pictured).

TOP 5

Classic LEGO set cameos in the movie

1 LEGO Pirates Brickbeard's Bounty (set 6243), 2009

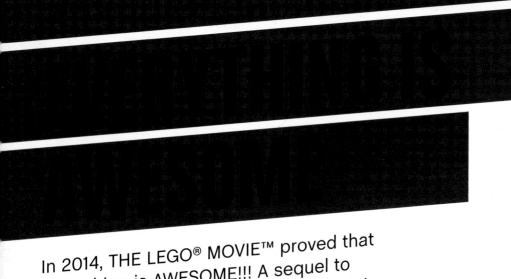

2 LEGO Castle King's Castle (set 70404), 2013

3 LEGO® Friends Sunshine Ranch (set 41039), 2014

4 LEGO FABULAND Cathy Cat's Fun Park (set 3676), 1989

5 LEGO Vikings Viking Ship Challenges the Midgard Serpent (set 7018), 2005

REALLY?!

Fan-made "brickfilm" Gorgy Wants a Horse won a competition to appear in THE LEGO MOVIE. It is in the sequence where everyone unleashes their building potential.

AWESOME!

When the *Millennium Falcon* appears, the voices of C-3PO and Lando Calrissian are provided by the same actors who play those characters in the live-action *Star Wars*™ saga.

WOW!

Two years before *Batman v Superman: Dawn of Justice*, THE LEGO MOVIE was the first time Batman and Superman appeared together on the big screen.

Brick History

Space minifigure Benny was based on one particular character that Chris Miller (one of THE LEGO MOVIE writer/directors) has owned since childhood, right down to his worn out printing and broken helmet.

SPACESHIP!

Piece particulars

Lord Business's cape is actually a life-sized businessman's tie! Toward the end of the movie, "the Man Upstairs" can be seen wearing one in the same color.

YOU SPEAK FRENCH, NOW?

WHAT'S IN A NAME?

One of the titles considered for THE LEGO MOVIE was "The Piece of Resistance." The phrase, used throughout the film, is a riff on "pièce de résistance," French for "the most important thing!"

BIG-SCREEN BATMAN

After LEGO® Batman got his big-screen debut in THE LEGO MOVIE, he got to star in his own movie with a supporting cast of heroes and villains.

> I DO ALL MY OWN STUNTS.

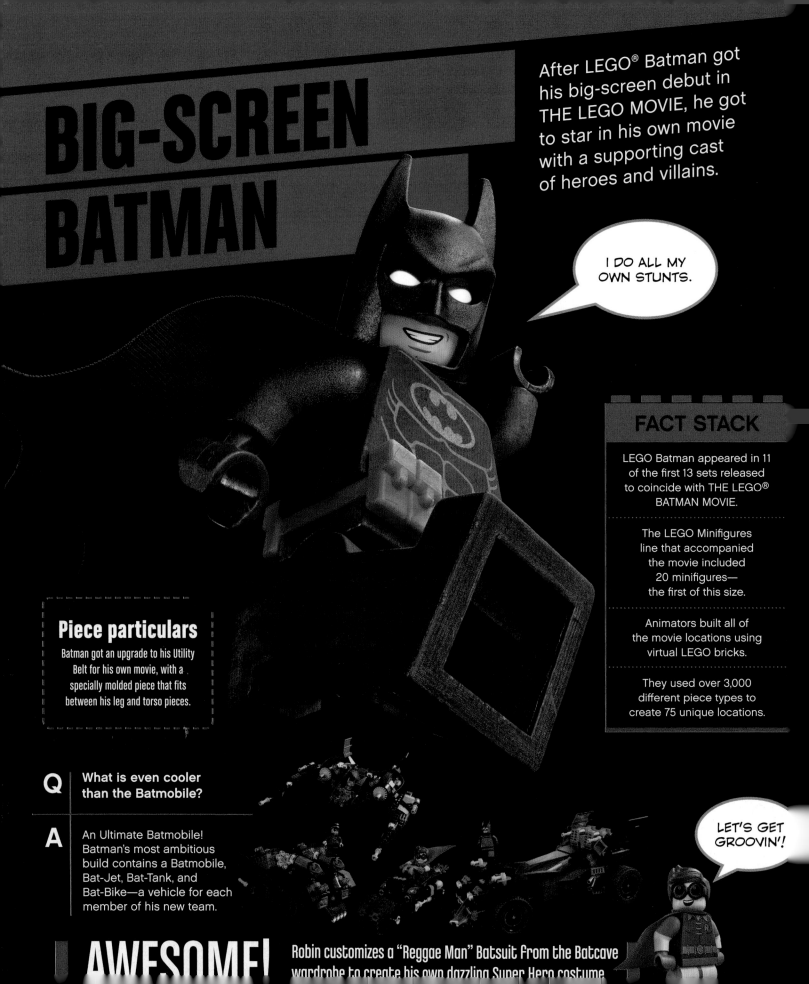

FACT STACK

LEGO Batman appeared in 11 of the first 13 sets released to coincide with THE LEGO® BATMAN MOVIE.

The LEGO Minifigures line that accompanied the movie included 20 minifigures— the first of this size.

Animators built all of the movie locations using virtual LEGO bricks.

They used over 3,000 different piece types to create 75 unique locations.

Piece particulars

Batman got an upgrade to his Utility Belt for his own movie, with a specially molded piece that fits between his leg and torso pieces.

Q What is even cooler than the Batmobile?

A An Ultimate Batmobile! Batman's most ambitious build contains a Batmobile, Bat-Jet, Bat-Tank, and Bat-Bike—a vehicle for each member of his new team.

> LET'S GET GROOVIN'!

AWESOME!

Robin customizes a "Reggae Man" Batsuit from the Batcave wardrobe to create his own dazzling Super Hero costume.

COSTUME CHANGES

Harley Quinn is a master of disguise, so it's no surprise she has many different looks in THE LEGO BATMAN MOVIE, from a tutu-clad rollerskater to a distinguished-looking doctor.

Tutu Harley

Roller Derby Harley

Nurse Harley

Doctor Quinzel

Brick History

Actor Billy Dee Williams played good guy Harvey Dent in the 1989 movie *Batman*, but not his villainous alter ego Two-Face. Williams now appears as the voice of minifigure Two-Face.

81

Number of muddy brown 1x1 round plates in Clayface Splat Attack (set 70904).

REALLY?!

Emmet built his friends a double-decker couch in THE LEGO MOVIE. It reappears on a grimy Gotham City street in THE LEGO BATMAN MOVIE.

LOOK CLOSER

Batman's foe Bane has an unusual decoration on his buggy: a teddy bear! It is a reference to the villains's favorite toy as a child.

WOW!

The movie's director, Chris McKay, has a Catwoman tattoo on his arm.

Brick statistics

Arkham Asylum
(set 70912)

1,628 pieces
Make up the secure facility set

236 pages
In the instruction booklet

12 minifigures
Including five inmates

2 of every food piece
Double sausages, donuts, watermelon slices, and pretzels

1 basketball hoop
For recreation time

SO NINJA!

Everyone's favorite ninja team span into cinemas in 2017, with the release of THE LEGO® NINJAGO MOVIE™. The ninja face new challenges, including life at Ninjago High School!

ANYONE WANT TO GO TO THE MOVIES?

Piece particulars

More than 30 new LEGO pieces were created for the movie, including restyled hair pieces for the ninja, helmets for their Shark Army foes, and new ninja weaponry.

FACT STACK

There were seven full seasons of the LEGO NINJAGO *Masters of Spinjitzu* TV show before the ninja made the move to the big screen.

Lord Garmadon returns to his evil ways in the movie, after being briefly good.

Kai appears in six of the first 13 movie tie-in sets—the most of any of the ninja.

A new range of LEGO® Minifigures contains 20 characters from the movie, including Lord Garmadon in his pajamas!

LOOK CLOSER

Cole's t-shirt features the name of rock band AC/DC, but it is written in the Ninjago language.

WE'RE A FISHY-LOOKING BUNCH.

TOP 5
Strangest Shark Army soldiers

1 **Great White Guy** (set 70609)

2 **Jellyfish Guy** (set 70614)

3 **Lobster Guy** (set 70614)

4 **Shark Guy** (set 70615)

5 **Angler Guy** (set 70616)

WORD ON THE STREET

Signs in Ninjago City are written in the Ninjago language, which was created especially for the movie. The Ninjago language is based on the Roman alphabet, but the symbols can be read left to right, top to bottom, or in clusters.

REALLY?!

It took animation company Animal Logic a whole year to build Ninjago City, a huge and complex virtual metropolis.

STARS OF THE SMALL SCREEN

From FABULAND to the Freemakers, NINJAGO ninjas to NEXO KNIGHTS™ heroes, LEGO characters have a long history of coming to life on TV and DVD.

1,100,000

US viewers tuned into the finale of LEGO® NEXO KNIGHTS® season one!

Q What was the first-ever LEGO TV show?

A Way back in 1987, the animals of LEGO FABULAND were made into clay figures for the stop-motion animated series *Edward and Friends*. It starred Edward the Elephant… and his friends!

TOP 5
Unmissable LEGO TV and DVD specials

1 LEGO *Atlantis: The Movie* (2010)

2 LEGO® *Star Wars™: The Padawan Menace* (2011)

3 LEGO *Star Wars: The Empire Strikes Out* (2012)

4 LEGO® *DC Comics Super Heroes: Batman Be-Leaguered* (2014)

5 LEGO® *Scooby-Doo™: Knight Time Terror* (2015)

Brick statistics

LEGO NINJAGO: *Masters of Spinjitzu*

74 regular episodes
Since 2011, divided into seven seasons

4 pilot episodes
Introducing the ninja for the first time

6 mini-episodes
Set between the pilots and season one

29 webisodes
Short bursts of story on LEGO.com

1 TV special
The 2016 epic, *Day of the Departed*

30 hours

IT'S A SIGN!

In the 2016 *Disney* XD miniseries LEGO *Star Wars: The Resistance Rises*, BB-8 disguises Poe Dameron's ship by slapping First Order stickers over the Alliance symbols!

REALLY?!

The 550th episode of *The Simpsons* is a special, digitally animated story, set in a world made enti...

KEY DATES

2005
LEGO *Star Wars* makes its TV debut in the animated short film LEGO *Star Wars: Revenge of the Brick*, shown on Cartoon Network.

2013
Legends of Chima: The Animated Series launches alongside the first LEGO Legends of Chima sets. It goes on to run for three seasons.

2015
Viewers get their first glimpse of the LEGO NEXO KNIGHTS TV series in December, just before the first sets launch in January 2016.

2016
Two new LEGO series launch on the Netflix streaming service—LEGO BIONICLE: *The Journey to One* and LEGO Friends: *The Power of Friendship*.

MEET THE FREEMAKERS

In 2016, LEGO *Star Wars: The Freemaker Adventures* was the first LEGO *Star Wars* TV series to focus on brand-new characters, rather than familiar faces from the movie saga.

Rowan Freemaker
A brave young boy who finds out he can use the Force.

R0-GR
The Freemakers' battered old battle droid— known as Roger!

Zander Freemaker
An ace pilot who flies the family ship, *StarScavenger*.

Kordi Freemaker
The brains behind the Freemakers' salvage business.

AWESOME!

LEGO NEXO KNIGHTS viewers can download NEXO Powers straight from the TV screen using the NEXO KNIGHTS app.

BRICKS AND PIXELS

LEGO video games combine timeless LEGO play and familiar minifigures with huge virtual worlds that could never be built in real life.

COME WITH ME TO LEGO ISLAND!

FIRST MINIFIGURE BASED ON A GAME

Infomaniac (set 2181)

REALLY?!

The LEGO Minifigures Gingerbread Man appears as a playable character in the LEGO NINJAGO: Shadow of Ronin video game.

I'M A GINGER NINJA!

DUNK ME!

KEY DATES

1997
LEGO® *Island* is the first ever LEGO PC game. On the island, players can build vehicles and meet friendly minifigures.

1999
LEGO® *Racers* was is the first LEGO game released for several different games consoles, and features motor-racing pirates, knights, and aliens.

2005
LEGO *Star Wars: The Video Game* takes LEGO gaming to a new level, with a storyline spanning the entire *Star Wars* prequel trilogy.

2008
LEGO *Batman: The Video Game* is the first licensed LEGO game to tell an original story, rather than adapting a movie plot.

2010
LEGO® *Universe* becomes the first LEGO multiplayer online game. In it, players use their building skills to save imagination itself.

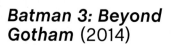

Batman 3: Beyond Gotham (2014)

32 voice actors
Including 1960s Batman actor, Adam West

150 built-in characters
Plus another 70 available for download

45 missions
Including zero-gravity outer-space action

28 playable vehicles
Plus 10 more available for download

8 Batsuits
Including Arctic, Space, and Scuba suits

SOLO VOCAL

The LEGO *Star Wars: The Force Awakens* game features brand new dialogue recorded by the stars of the movie. That means "Wookiee cookies" is one of the last things Harrison Ford will ever say as Han Solo!

LOOK CLOSER

UNIVERSE

The "U" in the logo for 2010's LEGO *Universe* game is a minifigure hand viewed from above.

IT'S A SIGN!

Clicking on this symbol in LEGO® *Worlds* lets you customize your minifigure avatar's head, hair, and clothes.

200+

Number of cars you can drive in 2013's LEGO® City *Undercover* video game.

WOW!

Want to see the world from a minifigure's point of view? LEGO *Worlds* includes a first-person play option for doing just that.

Brick History

THE LEGO MOVIE *Video Game* had the first game environment built entirely from virtual LEGO bricks—making it technically possible to build the game world for real!

FACT STACK

The first LEGO video game was LEGO® *Fun To Build*, released for the Sega Pico console in 1995.

Other early games included LEGO® *Chess* and city-building simulator, LEGO® *Loco*.

Since 2005, almost 30 LEGO video games have been made by developers TT Games.

There are dozens of LEGO mini-games to play for free on LEGO.com

AWESOME!

The 2017 "sandbox" game LEGO *Worlds* acts as an infinite LEGO collection that allows players to build anything they can imagine from an endless array of bricks.

BREAK THE RULES!

LEGO® DIMENSIONS™ is a video game launched in 2015 that brings real minifigures and LEGO sets to life in a digital world.

PRECIOUS MEDAL.

SCARIEST DIMENSIONS DOUBLE ACT

Gollum and Shelob (from *The Lord of the Rings*)

FACT STACK

LEGO DIMENSIONS is a game for up to two players.

You need a Starter Pack and a compatible games console to play.

Extension Packs let you add more adventures and characters over time.

Some Expansion Packs add battle arenas with four gameplay modes for up to four players.

Brick History

LEGO DIMENSIONS comes with a Starter Pack that includes a LEGO® Toy Pad to connect real LEGO minifigures, vehicles, and gadgets to the game.

THEY'RE MY RELATIVE DIMENSIONS!

DOCTOR, DOCTOR...

The LEGO DIMENSIONS minifigure of the Doctor from *Doctor Who* has only one face, but he can be used to play the game as any one of the character's 13 incarnations!

REALLY?!

Little is known about the evil LEGO DIMENSIONS villain Lord Vortech. He is so mysterious that no LEGO minifigures have ever been made of him.

Q | My Toy Pad is flashing! Why?

A | The LEGO DIMENSIONS Toy Pad lights up, flashes, and changes color to give players clues for solving puzzles, finding items, or to point characters in the right direction.

Piece particulars

The brick-built figure of BMO from the LEGO® DIMENSIONS™ *Adventure Time*™ Team Pack has blue sausage pieces for arms.

AWESOME!

In LEGO NINJAGO, Master Wu's Dragon (set 70734) is made from hundreds of pieces. In LEGO DIMENSIONS, the creature is recreated using fewer than 50.

WOW!

All DIMENSIONS packs includes a vehicle or gadget that can be built in three different ways, to unlock different in-game features.

REALLY?!

In their first in-game encounter, Batman mistakes Krusty the Clown from *The Simpsons* for his archenemy, the Joker!

WOW!

LEGO DIMENSIONS is at least the 80th time Sonic the Hedgehog has appeared in a video game—but the first time he has been turned into a minifigure.

SMART BUILDING

LEGO® MINDSTORMS® blends LEGO building and computer programming to create real-life robots, inspiring endless inventions from young engineers.

FAST FACTS

LEGO MINDSTORMS robots are programmed with easy-to-use, free LEGO software.

Each robot is brought to life using a LEGO MINDSTORMS Intelligent Brick.

Intelligent Bricks act on user instructions sent to them via infrared, Bluetooth, or Wi-Fi.

LEGO MINDSTORMS is the best-selling product in the history of the LEGO Group.

TOP 5

Robots that can be made with MINDSTORMS EV3 (set 31313)

1 The surefooted, bazooka-blasting, blade-spinning **EV3RSTORM**.

2 The handy, heavy-lifting, grab-and-go **GRIPP3R**.

3 The slithering, snake-like, superfast **R3PTAR**.

4 The snapping, shooting, six-legged **SPIK3R**.

5 The blasting, bashing, go-anywhere **TRACK3R**.

WOW!

LEGO MINDSTORMS is in the Carnegie Mellon University Robot Hall of Fame, alongside robots such as C-3PO, R2-D2, and WALL-E!

KEY DATES

1984
The LEGO Group partners with the Massachusetts Institute of Technology Media Laboratory to develop educational computer-controlled LEGO sets for schools.

1998
The LEGO MINDSTORMS Robotics Invention System (set 9719) introduces the programmable RCX (Robotic Command eXplorer) brick for building working robots!

2006
LEGO MINDSTORMS NXT (set 8527) makes LEGO robotics more powerful, but also easier to use, using the NXT Intelligent Brick.

2009
LEGO MINDSTORMS NXT 2.0 (set 8547) keeps LEGO robots at the cutting edge with new programming options and extra sensors.

3.256

Seconds taken by LEGO MINDSTORMS robot Cubestormer III to solve a Rubik's Cube.

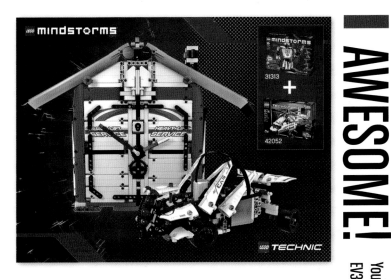

You can build a working cuckoo clock by combining LEGO MINDSTORMS EV3 with 2016's LEGO Technic Heavy Lift Helicopter (set 42052).

REALLY?!

In 2014, 12-year-old Shubham Banerjee used LEGO MINDSTORMS EV3 to build Braigo—the world's lightest, quietest, most cost-effective braille printer!

BRICK CHALLENGE

On LEGO.com/mindstorms there are more instructions for EV3 robots, including LEGO Technic combination builds. What robotic creation will you come up with?

Brick statistics

LEGO MINDSTORMS EV3 (set 31313)

357 LEGO Technic elements
For building robots up to 16 inches (41cm) tall!

1 EV3 Intelligent Brick
The control center of your MINDSTORMS robot

3 environmental sensors
Respond to color, touch, and infrared light

2 large servo motors
For powerful, precise movement

1 infrared beacon
To control your robot remotely

A LEAGUE OF THEIR OWN

In 2008, the LEGO Group and educational charity FIRST (For Inspiration and Recognition of Science and Technology) launched a LEGO MINDSTORMS competition for school students. Today, the *FIRST* LEGO® League has more than 32,000 school teams worldwide.

2013
LEGO MINDSTORMS EV3 (set 31313) takes LEGO programming to the next level, with complete control from your smartphone or tablet.

2017
LEGO BOOST (set 17101) brings coding to a younger audience with buildable, programmable characters such as Vernie the Robot and Frankie the Cat.

JOIN THE CLUB!

For years, the official LEGO® Club delighted millions of members around the world, and in 2017 it became LEGO Life, a growing community of fans of all ages.

FACT STACK

In 2017, the former LEGO Club was rebranded as LEGO Life.

LEGO Life is a free club for LEGO fans in 25 countries around the world.

Members can sign up for a magazine and email updates.

LEGO Life is a free social app full of LEGO videos, building challenges, quizzes, and more.

WOW!

There were more than 30 different versions of the former LEGO Club magazine published in 10 different languages around the world.

TOP 5
Former LEGO Club cartoon mascots

1 Max (2007)

2 The Amazing Redini (2002)

3 Zack the LEGO Maniac (1989)

4 Brick and Bridget Bildmore (1987)

Every issue of LEGO *Life* magazine is packed full of comics, puzzles, building ideas, pictures of reader's very best builds, and more.

Q Are there LEGO clubs for older builders?

A Yes, there are adult fan communities all around the world. The oldest such "LEGO User Group" is De Bouwsteen ("The Building Block") in the Netherlands.

READ ALL ABOUT IT!

Over the years, the various LEGO Club magazines included *Brick Kicks*, *Bricks 'n Pieces*, LEGO *Mania Magazine*, and LEGO *Tech Torque*, which was especially for LEGO Technic fans.

Piece particulars

In 2010, the former LEGO Club's cartoon mascot, Max, was made into a real minifigure (set 852996), featuring all exclusive parts.

Brick History

In 1963, Snap, "The fun book for LEGO Club members," launched in the USA. The first official LEGO Club was set up in Canada three years later.

5 Johnny and Jane LEGO (1963)

REALLY?!

If every former LEGO Club member joined hands, the line would stretch all the way from the USA to Russia!

1

2

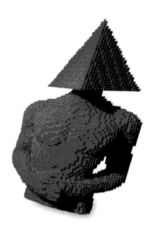

3

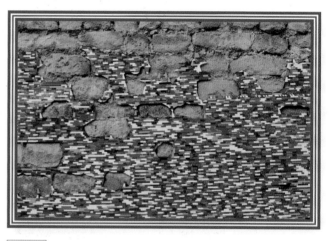

4

THE ART OF

Notable LEGO artworks

1 **Paul Hetherington** won the Best in Show award at LEGO fan event BrickCon 2015 for his mechanical "steampunk love story" sculpture, "Unchain My Heart."

2 **Vesa Lehtimäki** uses sets and minifigures from the LEGO *Star Wars* theme to compose photographs full of action, wit, and atmosphere.

3 Since 2004, **Nathan Sawaya** has worked as a full-time LEGO artist, and has toured the world with his exhibition "The Art of the Brick."

4 "Dispatchwork" is a collaborative art project devised by **Jan Vormann** in which LEGO bricks are used to fill cracks and voids in damaged walls.

5 In 2012, street artist **Megx** painted a disused rail bridge in Wuppertal, Germany, to look as if it were made from giant LEGO bricks.

6 "The Collectivity Project" is a touring art installation by **Olafur Eliasson.** It invites visitors to rebuild a vast LEGO city according to their own vision.

BUILDING

5

6

7

8

7   **Mike Doyle** builds elaborate,
     tumbledown LEGO houses, which
     he photographs for limited-edition
     art prints before taking them
     apart and starting again.

8   **Sean Kenney** is a professional
     artist who creates LEGO sculpture.
     His latest exhibition, "Nature
     Connects," features more than 100
     lifelike LEGO animals and plants.

TOP 5

LEGO online game categories

1 **Action games**, such as LEGO NINJAGO *Skybound*.

2 **Strategy games**, such as LEGO® *Bits and Bricks*.

3 **Adventure games**, such as LEGO NEXO KNIGHTS *Super Mega Power Panic*.

4 **Creative games**, such as LEGO Friends *Art Maker*.

5 **Preschool games**, such as LEGO® Juniors *Fire Truck*.

REALLY?!

In 2015, the LEGO Facebook page invited fans to build and upload an image of a Kronkiwongi— whatever that is!

ONE-STOP SHOP

Customers at the LEGO Shop area of LEGO.com can buy everything from huge, hard-to-find LEGO Creator Expert sets to individual elements using the Pick A Brick service.

AREN'T I JUST CONQUIST-ADORABLE!

FIRST LEGO INSTAGRAM STAR

Conquistador

CHOOSE LIFE

LEGO Life is a free app for smartphones and tablets that lets you share your best builds, take on building challenges, and chat with other fans using special LEGO emojis!

You have to be 13 or older to use most third-party social media sites

WOW!

There are lots of seasonal building ideas on the official LEGO Pinterest page, including a Thanksgiving turkey!

LOOK CLOSER

If you scroll to the bottom of LEGO.com and click on "Building Instructions," you'll find a searchable database of booklets for building thousands of LEGO sets.

4,039

The number of years it would take one person to watch all the videos viewed on the LEGO YouTube channel in 2015!

Brick statistics

12 million likes
On the official LEGO Facebook page

2.5 million subscribers
To the official LEGO YouTube channel

1.9 million followers
Of @LEGO on Instagram

435,000 followers
Of @LEGO_Group on Twitter

FACT STACK

LEGO.com is available in 19 international editions, from Dutch to Turkish.

Every month, almost 18 million people visit LEGO.com from locations around the world.

More than five million pages have gone live on LEGO.com since it launched in 1996.

Most visitors to LEGO.com return to the site on a daily basis to see what's new.

BRICKS AND CLICKS

RECORD-BREAKING BRICKS

There really are no limits when it comes to LEGO building, as these remarkable record setters and smashers all set out to show!

AM I TOO LATE TO JOIN?

The **longest LEGO brick sculpture** ever made was a 5,179ft (1,579m) millipede built out of 2,901,760 bricks over the course of two months in 2005. Thousands of families contributed to the creepy-crawly at a shopping mall in Italy, in an event organized by Consorzio Esercenti CC.

LONGEST LEGO SCULPTURE

In 2008, LEGO Group employees in the UK assembled an army of 35,210 LEGO *Star Wars* clone troopers to create the **largest display of LEGO minifigures** ever seen! The troopers were arranged in just six and a half hours to raise money for UK charity the National Autistic Society.

FASTEST BRICK STACK

The world record for **most LEGO bricks built onto a baseplate in 30 seconds** is currently 127 bricks. The record was set by Kamil Dominowski from Poland at a 2015 LEGO fan event held in the UK. How many bricks can you add to a baseplate in just 30 seconds?

LARGEST MINIFIGURE DISPLAY

In May 2013, the record for the world's **longest LEGO railway** was set by Henrik Ludvigsen and more than 80 other LEGO fans in Denmark. It took a battery-powered LEGO train almost four hours to travel the 2.5-mile (4km) route, which was made from more than 93,000 LEGO elements!

LONGEST RAILWAY TRACK

The world record for **most assembled LEGO sets in one private collection** was set by Kyle Ugone in 2011. At the time, his array of built sets totaled 1,091 and was kept at his home in Arizona, USA, where it had been accumulating since 1986!

The world's **largest LEGO airplane** was shown at the World's largest LEGO show in Krakow, Poland. The model of the US Presidential aircraft, *Air Force One*, measures 36ft (11m) long and 9ft (3m) high and is about 1/6 the size of the real thing.

The world's **largest LEGO house** was assembled in the UK by 1,200 volunteers as part of a BBC TV series. The finished two-story structure had four life-sized rooms, including a kitchen and a bathroom, and stood 15ft (4.6m) tall.

The LEGO Group broke its own world record for building the **tallest LEGO tower** in 2015! Around 18,000 volunteers contributed to the 114ft (35m) tower in Italy, which comprised more than half a million bricks. The tower took five days to complete, and was built to raise money for an environmental charity.

THE WORLD'S BIGGEST LEGO® SCULPTURE: TOWER BRIDGE

In September 2016, this giant model of London's Tower Bridge was declared the new world-record holder as the world's largest LEGO sculpture.

5,805,846 bricks
Weighing 45,980lbs (20,865kg)

28 LEGO builders
Worked on the project, including LEGO Certified Professional Duncan Titmarsh, founder of the company Bright Bricks

42ft (13m) high
And 144ft (44m) wide

29 times taller
Than the LEGO Tower Bridge set (10214)

7 months to build
And a year to develop from start to finish

INDEX

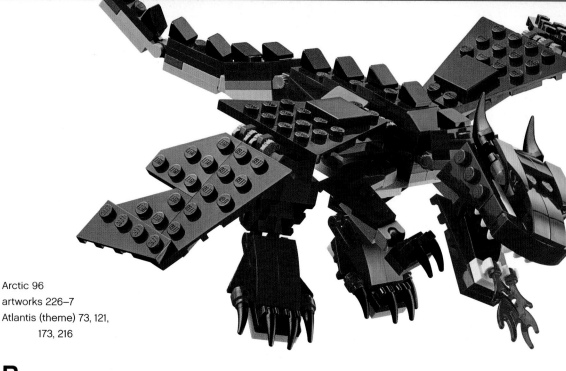

ACKNOWLEDGMENTS

The publisher would like to thank the following for their kind permission to reproduce their photographs:

Picture library credits:

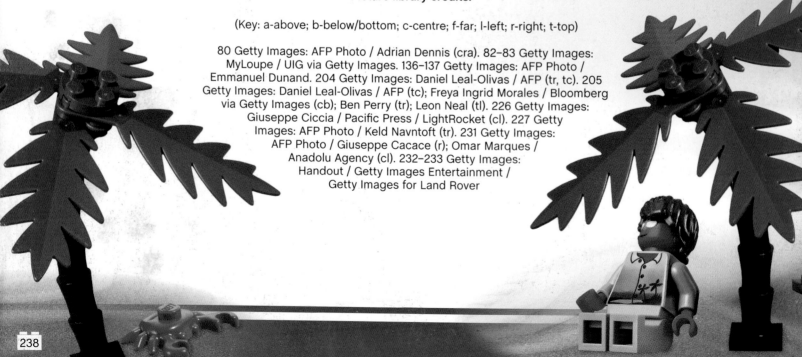

**DK would also like to thank the following people
for their help in producing this book:**

Signe Wiese, Kristian Reimer Hauge, Camilla Pedersen, Jan Ryaa, and the
many designers at the LEGO Group who contributed additional insider facts
• Randi Sørensen, Paul Hansford, Martin Leighton Lindhardt, and Heidi K.
Jensen at the LEGO Group for their roles in bringing this book to fruition •
Joel Baker for the use of his LEGOLAND Florida photography • Jan Vormann,
Sean Kenney, Mike Doyle, Megx, Paul Hetherington, and Vesa Lehtimäki for
allowing us to feature images of their LEGO artworks.

 Penguin Random House

Senior Editor Hannah Dolan
Senior Designer Lauren Adams
Editors Ellie Rose and Beth Davies
Editorial Assistants Natalie Edwards and Joseph Stewart
Designers Elena Jarmoskaite, Gema Salamanca, and Rhys Thomas
Senior Pre-production Producer Marc Staples
Senior Producer Louise Daly
Managing Editor Paula Regan
Managing Art Editor Jo Connor
Publisher Julie Ferris
Art Director Lisa Lanzarini
Publishing Director Simon Beecroft

Additional writers Rod Gillies and Caylin Malloy

First American Edition, 2017
Published in the United States by DK Publishing
345 Hudson Street, New York, New York 10014
DK, a Division of Penguin Random House LLC

17 18 19 20 21 10 9 8 7 6 5 4 3 2

002–280844–Sep/2017

Page design © 2017 Dorling Kindersley Limited.

A catalog record for this book is available from
the Library of Congress.

ISBN: 978-1-4654-6411-8

DK books are available at special discounts when purchased in bulk for sales promotions,
premiums, fund-raising, or educational use. For details, contact: DK Publishing Special Markets,
345 Hudson Street, New York, New York 10014
SpecialSales@dk.com

Printed and bound in China

A WORLD OF IDEAS:
SEE ALL THERE IS TO KNOW
www.dk.com
www.LEGO.com